How Dads can make a difference

Papa Kubs

Dedication

To my awesome wife and three amazing children,

Each of you has played a significant part in challenging me and helping me become a better man, husband, father, family member and friend. The life experiences in this book help me see just how wonderful life is having all of you in it! In writing about these events, I realize how quickly life passes us by if we don't stop and pay attention. Kids, each of you has grown into a wonderful young adult; you bring me joy. I look forward in awe and wonder of what you'll do next. I am proud to be called your husband and dad and to call you my wife and children.

Papa Kubs

How Dads can make a difference

ISBN: 978-0-692-86595-8
Printed in the United States of America

Credits
Cover Design and Layout by Jody Kunz Clark, Studio 810
Edited by Liz Wheeler
Photography by Sandy Jones Photography

Publisher
Tom Kubinski Publishing DBA Papa Kubs
16955 39th Place North
Plymouth, Minnesota 55446

For additional books or quantity discounts, contact:
Tom "Papa Kubs" Kubinski
Phone: (612) 760-3700
Email: papakubs1@gmail.com

Contents

Part 2: The College Years

Appendix

Acknowledgements

This book is only possible because of a few people in my life that made me see the light or the changes that needed to be made in my life.

I was on a downward spiral. I was being consumed by all I wanted in life and all that I felt I needed to accomplish, do, and become. I was in self-destruct mode. I had all the treasures I needed right in front of me and did not realize it.

Luckily, I experienced some significant things that woke me up, and I want to thank:

My wife. Katie saw in me the man I was meant to be, could be, and was trying to be. Each time I got close, I would self-destruct and do or say things that took me further from my goal. She deserved better. I am truly in her debt for her willingness to stay and keep helping me grow into my potential. She is a GREAT MOM and truly knows how to nurture with her caring personality. That applies not only to our kids, but the biggest kid of them all, me! I said many times, "I am never growing up!" Thanks for believing in me, Katie; you are an AMAZING woman and, as I have often said after I became clean and sober, **"Yes, Dear. I love you, and I'm a very lucky man!"**

The police officer who pulled me over and helped me wake up by not letting me talk my way out of a DUI [driving under the influence], which caused me to visit my first AA [Alcoholics Anonymous] meeting the next night. It was there that I realized I had so many AWESOME things in my life to lose: a wonderful wife, three great children, including a newborn, a new house for all of us to start a truly great life of memories in, and a new job. I am PROUD to say, that I am a PROUD member of Bill's AA club and have been for over 16 years as of this writing.

My AA sponsor, who helped guide me through all that needed to be done in order for me to truly move forward in the most healthy and positive way in my new life. Sadly, he passed before this book was published. Since he had been a book store owner, I wanted him to be a part of it more than ever. Each of us needs someone, a mentor or friend, like this no matter who we are—someone who truly knows us, calls us out when needed, guides us to reconsider things in a different light, helps us to stop focusing on ourselves. We are here for others and not our own selfish concerns. Thanks for your guidance, Gary; I will never forget you!

My three gifts from God: Alexa, Tori and Collin. You three have truly allowed me to see just what it is to be a dad, how truly awesome it is, and all the fun things we can experience together. You've also been patient as we've learned how to handle difficulties together when they arise, how to be a team and how to be there for each other. I don't think I would have truly been ready or known what to do in many circumstances if not for your unconditional love. As I look back at photos of things we have done together, your smiles bring me right back to those special moments in time.

My Mom and Dad who showed me all that life could offer. I was able to experience MANY things in my life that MANY will never be able to. I was able to travel the world and see and experience life with those who had more and those who had nothing, which really opened my mind to helping others. They helped me excel in sports, to become a six-time All American Swimmer who set the 50-free record in the Minnesota Intercollegiate Athletic Conference as a freshman in college. They pushed me in directions that I would not have otherwise gone.

My father-in-law and mother-in-law who showed me how to be a better man, father and husband, and how to consider others before myself. They have given us so much with no expectations in return.

Because of all of these significant people in my life and these events, I was able to change the path I was on and realize that life was NOT all about me and what I wanted, needed and desired. It allowed me to become a better man, husband, father, friend, family member, co-worker, etc. I am eternally grateful and wish to say thanks to each and every one of you.

Prologue

We go through life at a much-too-fast, whirlwind pace and forget what it is truly all about. It's not about work, paying bills, getting that next sale, buying that next toy, or planning the most awesome vacation.

It's about having a positive impact on others through every day events. For me, that was most true when it came to the lives of my kids. And through it all, I realize that it's the little things that add up and make a big difference in not only their lives but also their friends' lives. In return, my life was impacted by them, helping me ultimately become a better man, father, husband and friend.

This compilation of short stories is both a life and family story as told from my perspective. It includes things I've done for (and to) my children—Alexa, Tori and Collin—through various ages and stages of life. Perhaps this book will provide you with a little push in the right direction and some creative ideas to make sure that impact is positive. I hope you find, as I did when I started doing these, that even better ideas pop into your mind, and each one is better than the last.

One of the biggest compliments came from my son when he said that his friends LOVE me and all the crazy, odd and fun things I do—even through the tough love and cold shower threats. So read, enjoy, laugh, cry, and try out some of these ideas—and then add your own!

Part 1

The Early Years

Chapter 1
Discipline.
Careful, You May Get Wet

There was a big difference between how I was disciplined as a child and how my wife was disciplined. At my house, we were spanked and got grounded. On the other hand, my wife grew up with warnings and talks. When we got married, we had to find a form of discipline with which we were both comfortable.

Our first method incorporated both the verbal and physical discipline. It told the kids where they were at in the discipline process and what was coming next if the negative behavior wasn't stopped.

Three warnings were given. We said:

- This is your first warning, please stop doing XYZ so it doesn't get to warning number two.

- This is your second warning, please stop doing XYZ so it doesn't get to warning number three.

- This is your THIRD and FINAL warning, please stop XYZ, otherwise you will get disciplined.

The discipline may have been a spanking or getting grounded or something else appropriate.

Well, this worked up to a certain age for each of them.

However, when Alexa got into her teenage years, spanking didn't seem appropriate or effective.

I was stumped when it seemed that no traction was being made, and I pondered what I could do or try next.

Being in sales, I was always reading, watching or participating in some type of self-improvement program, series, books or seminars. While attending one of Tony Robbins' seminars (where I actually walked on fire and did not get burned, totally a COOL and wonderful experience as was the seminar), he had a lady come up on stage and showed us a method that made me say HMMMMM.

This woman was going through a very emotionally upsetting situation. When she first got on stage, she was happy. But as soon as Tony got into her situation, she started to sink in her chair and cry. As she was talking, out of the blue, Tony threw a glass of water on her to change her state. As you can imagine, she looked surprised and shocked, and they both laughed when talking about it. Then he asked her again about the situation, and she went immediately back into the depressed, sunken, crying mode. Once again, Tony threw a glass of water on her, and she began to laugh again. After asking her for the third time about her situation, she laughed and didn't discuss it.

I decided, unbeknownst to my wife or kids, that I was going to try this "CHANGE the state" method with my kids at the next opportune time. And then it happened.

Alexa and I were having a discussion about the three warnings, and it was yielding no change at all. In fact, she was getting more difficult.

I then told her that, if she kept up this behavior, "I am going to pick you up and carry you to the shower and give you a COLD shower until your attitude changes regardless of what you have on or in your pockets." At this time, our kids did not have cell phones, so I was not too worried about anything like that being ruined. This announcement still brought about little change and neither she nor the other two kids believed I would do it.

After giving her the three warnings, I walked over to her quickly. As she started to move away from me, her eyes got bigger and bigger as she realized I was not kidding. Tori and Collin watched in disbelief or perhaps glee. I'm not sure which.

I picked her up and, as we headed up the stairs, told her she may want to remove anything from her pockets that she didn't want to get wet. We made it to the kids' bathroom despite her grabbing at door frames to prevent the inevitable. I turned the shower on as COLD as it would go and held her there for about two or three minutes.

She screamed, mad as you can imagine.

Tori, Collin, and I laughed, as you can imagine. I also told her this was the new norm, so she shouldn't push it.

Suddenly, Alexa started to laugh as well, and the discipline was over. After Alexa dried off and changed, the four of us continued the discussion on how discipline was going to change at our house.

I don't think I ever had to give Alexa another cold shower; however, Tori received one shortly after.

On the flip side, Collin was very young at this point and wanted me to give him one. So he purposely began to misbehave, but nothing was bad enough to warrant it. But it dawned on me that, at the rate he was going, he just might do something that justified it, and that is not what I wanted. The next time he went through three warnings, Collin got his cold shower. Now it was complete: three kids and three cold showers. Or so I thought.

Collin seemed to enjoy it and pushed it a few more times, so I took it to the next level and put him in the bathtub where he sat in COLD water for quite a bit longer. It seemed to squelch his desire for more.

These events became legend amongst my kids' friends. The girl's friends looked at me with fear and wonder while my son's friends all seemed to think it was a grand idea. In fact, Collin started to say to me in front of them, "He needs a cold shower," and the boys would all laugh.

On occasion, my son's friends did receive some form of the cold shower treatment. The kitchen faucet with the spray hose worked the best and laughs all around were experienced. It seemed to help in establishing a fun and respectful relationship with Collin and his friends. Our kids and their friends seemed to really enjoy our home where it was known to be a SAFE and FUN place to be.

Chapter 2
I will Fix That?

When Collin was very young, about seven or so, we were playing a game of copycat. We were running all around the house and what he did, I did. Down the stairs to the basement, around the couches we went, drop-tuck and rolling across the carpet (what you're supposed to do if you're on fire: stop, drop and roll), up the stairs, around the kitchen table and up to his room. When he got there, he ran around his mother who was putting his laundry away and did a swan dive onto his trundle bed. Wouldn't you know, I did the same. I guess I should have heeded my wife's comment just before I did it, "I wouldn't if I were you." The bed splintered since it was made of particle board.

Collin was laughing hysterically, while my wife was not. (Oh, if looks could kill!) "Nice," my wife responded. "Now what are you going to do?"

"Well, I can fix that?" I said uncertainly. What you need to know, though, is that if it can't be duct-taped, I can't fix it. My wife, knowing this about me, uttered something along the lines of disbelief.

However, I am resourceful, and I can take things apart. So I took one of each section and drove to the hardware store to see if we could salvage his bed thereby avoiding him sleeping on the floor and buying a whole new bed.

As I walked into the home improvement store loaded down with all these bits and pieces, "Rick" asked me what I needed help with. Rick was a little older than me and definitely had more handyman knowledge. I told him the saga along with the fact that both my wife and I were expecting me to fail.

"Tom, this is particle board, and we most certainly have this," he said before responding with what I thought was keen insight. "However, do you expect you will be playing this game in the future?"

After giving it a moment's thought, I said, "Now, that is an excellent question, and I most certainly do expect we will be doing the same thing sometime down the line!"

He said, "Then we should use number two knotty pine instead!" He then proceeded to cut the pine boards to size and pre-drilled the holes for me so all I needed to do was put the screws back in the holes.

I drove home and proceeded to put Collin's bed together. When it was all done, I called my wife and son up to his room.

"Ok, here it is done and put back together," I said. "Collin, give it a jump and see what happens."

He did, and it was solid. So, you can only guess what I did next, right? I proceeded to jump on it myself, and my wife shouted, "No, don't!"

To all of our disbelief, it was solid and held up perfectly. My wife said, "I am impressed and didn't think you could do it!!"

"What, you doubted me?" Little did she know, I was in just as much shock as she was!

Was all of this hassle worth it? I can honestly say, YES! It's only a bed, and the memories are sometimes worth inconveniences!

So, enjoy the many inconveniences. You and your kids will sit back and laugh about them for years to come. Even after many years, when you have forgotten them, you'll be sitting around the dinner table or out on the deck, and one of your kids will say, "Do you remember the time....?" Then all of a sudden, you are all right back there laughing hysterically. You will share those memories for a lifetime with many others, and they will be passed down to their kids and to new families.

Chapter 3
360s, Co-pilots and Squirrels

After a great weekend at Wisconsin Dells, my family and one of Collin's friends were driving back home. Our Denali was packed to the rafters with our supplies, and everyone was tired from the busy weekend and the long ride. As we were driving down our block and into our cul-de-sac, I decided I wanted to play just a little more before it was all over. So, I started to do 360s with our SUV. My wife, the co-pilot, didn't find my spontaneity in any way fun, funny or right.

However, each of my kids, Alexa, Tori, Collin, along with Grant, thought it was hysterical. Seeing as I'm a kid at heart, I am not sure if they truly liked it as much as I did or if they were just laughing at how much my wife was not having any part of it.

On the third or fourth rotation, my wife stopped worrying about what the neighbors were thinking and gave into how much fun it actually was.

Every so often, my kids will request the 360s by slyly saying, "Dad, do it!" when we have new victims in the car...or friends who have heard about it but want to experience it for themselves. Good times!

The Co-pilot Seat and Duties

In our car, the person in the front passenger seat is known as the co-pilot. And this title has some responsibilities determined by me, of course.

As co-pilot, you must cater to the needs of the pilot such as getting him something to eat or drink. Never, ever, in any circumstance, touch the radio. The co-pilot, of course, must be good company for the pilot so the co-pilot is not allowed to text or make phone calls. They also must stay alert and look out for police cars. Basically, the rules are made to mess with them!

When Collin was about fifteen, we were driving home from a hockey tournament with him and five of his friends. Collin was the co-pilot. Within two miles of leaving the arena, Collin had failed in his duties. There, on the side of the highway, was a police car, and Collin had not alerted me.

I said, "Not only were you on your phone, which is against the rules and duties of the copilot, but you failed to see and notify me of the police officer that is right there!" Once we had passed the officer, I pulled over on the side of the road and told Collin he was out as co-pilot; one of his friends could replace him.

Mandy in back jumped into the seat wholeheartedly, relishing this prestigious position. I asked her if she knew the rules and duties. She confirmed with a resounding yes and repeated them back to me.

So, I decided to test her. "Why don't you text your dad to let him know we are on our way home?" I asked. "No!" she immediately replied. "That's against the rules!"

"Well done," I replied. "You are far better at this than Collin!"

Squirrel

Of course, another rule for the vehicle is to always buckle up.

I don't know if you ever saw the movie *Up*, but it is an awesome kids' movie. One character is a dog named Doug with a short attention span who is easily distracted, especially by squirrels.

As I was heading out one time with my kids and a few of their friends, I noticed they hadn't buckled their seat belts. After leaving the cul-de-sac, I slammed on the breaks and yelled, "Squirrel!" A few of them were jostled forward and, surprisingly, actually looked for the squirrel. Eventually they figured out it was my way of saying, "Buckle up!" and they laughed and buckled up.

Needless to say, they all buckle up when they get into the car, and if they are not quick about it, I yell, "Squirrel!" and pump the breaks a little.

From time to time, they do taunt me by not being buckled just to see if I notice. I know who to watch for, and it has become a game. Yet, there are those who have heard but not experienced this exciting event for themselves and seem to purposefully not buckle so they can.

"Squirrel!" can be a good and fun thing! As long as it is done in a safe manner, donchaknow. [That disclaimer was for my wife's sake. Okay, maybe all moms needed that to be added for we dads can sometimes take things too far?]

Chapter 4
It's Tradition, Donchaknow*

One winter, our newly transplanted neighbors from Texas were experiencing their first Minnesota snowfall by sitting in their house in shorts. Their two sons were playing, and Mom and Dad were sitting by the fireplace watching TV with a glass of wine in hand.

Meanwhile, I put on my full winter outdoor ensemble (in Minnesota, this includes clothing that covers pretty much every square inch of skin) and walked on over to their house. After being received into their home, I asked, "What are you guys doing?"

Rich looked at me and said the family was relaxing and enjoying the weather.

I said, "Well, its tradition on the first Minnesota snowfall to get out and go sledding!"

His two boys jumped up and down with enthusiasm. "Yeah, let's go, Dad!"

Rich hastened to inform me that they didn't have any sleds and therefore wouldn't be able to do it.

Well, I informed him right back that we just happened to have quite a few sleds, so all he needed to do was put down the wine, get bundled up in snow gear, and he'd be good to go!

He hemmed and hawed while the boys kept pestering him about wanting to go.

After about five minutes, he finally gave in and I said, "Great, just meet us in my back yard, and we will see you then."

It took about 30 minutes for him and his boys to show up in our back yard, and he was not too keen on it from the looks of it. My three kids and I were sitting by the portable fire pit with the sleds sitting beside us. Rich then asked, "Where are we going to slide?"

I said, "Right over there."

We have a small berm in our backyard with a bunch of evergreen trees. The hill is about five feet tall and has a gradual slope to it. You need to fit between one set of trees to have any type of slide, but it isn't much, I must say.

Rich says, "Really?"

I said, "You betcha!"

We all headed up to the top of the berm, even my three kids who have no idea what is going on because, despite what I told Rich, we'd never done it before! I just wanted to mess with Rich.

I sent each one of my three down the hill one by one, then sent his two boys down the hill followed by myself and then Rich.

After all seven of us had done one slide down the very small hill, I said, "Okay, that's great. Now we're done. Our first snow, and the sledding adventure is complete!" And I headed toward our house.

As I was walking into the house, Rich said, with disbelief, something like, "You've got to be kidding me! I went through all the work of dressing up after sitting comfortably in my house by fireplace and TV with glass in hand and this is it?"

I said, "Yep, that's what you do on the first snowfall. Have a great night!" Rich sat there like a deer caught in the headlights, but who could blame him? He had no idea!

I did go in, but my kids and his stayed out and continued to slide for a bit longer. You see, it was Rich's kids' first snowfall and sledding experience, so they didn't know any better, and my kids just thought it was great.

It was classic, and he never let me forget it once he found out I was playing him.

The kids thought it was hilarious!

Remember, its tradition. Donchaknow.

What are your newly inspired traditions, especially with those not from around your neck of the woods? Have fun with them, and those will be memories that you, your kids and those you play them on will not forget!

*Translated "don't you know" and pronounced Don't Cha Know in the Tom Kubinski Polish and Minnesota way.

Chapter 5
The Negotiator

Tori is not only our second child but our second daughter as well. To say that she is strong willed, independent and a go-getter is an understatement! She knows what she wants and goes after it. She simply will not take no for an answer but needs you to tell her exactly why not. Simply saying, "Because I'm the dad, that's why" won't work. She'll have none of that.

When Tori was young, she wanted some candy; she came up to us and asked if she could have two or three pieces. Surprisingly, she didn't just ask for a single treat. She left herself room for negotiation! Because of her tender age, this tells you this was nature, not nurture! She was self-taught!

She then came back with, "How about one or two?"

We responded in the negative.

"How about just one then?"

The answer was still no.

"Why not?"

Well, it wasn't before a meal time or anything like that. She hadn't had many before either. I don't recall the exact reason why we were saying no and, to be honest with you, we couldn't come up with a solid reason and came back with, "Because we are your mother and father, and we said no."

"Why not?" she again asked, pushing for a more sound reason. Ultimately, we gave in; we couldn't come up with a good reason, and she has not let up since.

Keep it up, Tori Boo, as I call her. You'll make it big in this world by making sure you get what you want, how you want it and when you want it. If someone doesn't give it, you'll be sure to ask them "Why NOT?" and they'd better have a sound reason for you!

A huge smile comes to my face as I look back at the many times Tori has pushed both Katie and I for all those answers. I know she will truly be a success in life as she stands her ground and won't allow herself or her mission to simply be brushed off.

So dads, be prepared. It isn't all that easy to just say no anymore. You'll need to be prepared to verbalize your reasons even when you might not be prepared for those strong willed, independent and self-assured women you are raising. Keep in mind that they will go far in life with these traits!

Chapter 6
The Girl Scout Cookie Dad

Our girls were enrolled in what I feel is a very important self-discovery and empowering program. The Girls Scouts! The very first time I took them door to door to sell cookies, I watched both of our little scared girls walk timidly up to their first door to ask if the resident wanted to buy cookies. They rang the doorbell, probably hoping no one answered the door.

When the door was answered, the girls went into the presentation that we had rehearsed many times so they had an idea of what to say, and I was nearby just in case they needed help, but they didn't.

Alexa knocked on the first door, Tori the second, and back and forth. This way, the sales opportunities were fair and it allowed each of them to see what the other did and experienced along the way.

The person greeted them with a smile and usually said something like, "I'm so glad you stopped by, I've been waiting for someone to come to my door so I could order them. I'll take...."

Wow! The girls were so excited and wanted to go to the next door and the next and next. Almost everyone that answered ordered something from them unless they had already ordered.

Sales is possibly the hardest job in the world! Yet most of us don't sell a product that everyone wants, looks forward to and loves to eat! So, these sales are really much easier than all the other fundraisers I ever did. But for the girls, it was a first time experience with all the uncertainties and terror that accompanies that. Boy, did they overcome that quickly!

For the chance at the most success, I took them to townhomes where you could walk a little ways, be more protected from the elements and hit a lot of households quickly. Don't get me wrong, we did do single homes as well. You can't overlook them donchaknow!

Well, our order form was full and now all we had to do was wait for the cookies to be made and shipped so we could pick them up and deliver them and learn how to handle the money.

Delivery day finally came and I made this a family event sans Katie. We packed our van to the roof with the cookies making sure that our son Collin could easily reach each kind of cookie. Then we all drove to the first townhome.

Our finely tuned sales and delivery organization was about to pay off! The girls looked at the address, told Collin what they needed, and figured out the cost. Then the girls delivered the cookies, accepted payment, gave change and thanked the customers for their order.

After the first one, both Alexa and Tori came running back to the van and couldn't wait to get to the next door, which was right next door. We tackled the deliveries in record time. All four of us had an awesome time and couldn't wait until next year to do it all again.

Because I made this a family event, I became known as the Cookie Dad of the Girl Scouts. I was even written up in their *Bridge* newsletter! They came out and interviewed Alexa, Tori and even me. Who'd have thought that, right? They took pictures of us and everything.

So dads, let this story "bridge" your apprehension of door-to-door drudgery and make it a fun family event!

Chapter 7
The Fun Zone

If you can make your home be the fun (and safe) zone where the kids all want to hang out, you know you have done a great thing. It also allows you a chance to observe who they are playing with and watch them all grow up. So many other great things occur during these times as well.

Our house was one of these fun havens. First, we set some ground rules, which were:

- **NO** drinking

- **NO** drugs

- **NO** fighting

- Have fun and be safe

Then we got creative.

Summer Fun

When my kids were very young, we had a Rainbow swing set with a tire swing, slide, monkey bars and platform. I took cinder blocks and raised up the slide, then put a see-through, rectangular, knee-high, blow-up pool at its edge. Finally, I ran a hose on top of the platform above the slide and voila! Our own makeshift water slide. The kids LOVED it and had hours of fun with their friends and us.

As the kids got older, we progressed to an even larger, above-ground pool that held 18,000 gallons of water. It was usually situated at the side of the yard, and you needed a ladder to get into and out of it. When they were little, we'd put life jackets on them, and then we would all run in a circle to create a whirlpool. Then we would simply stop and let the current move us all in a circle for what seemed like hours on end. When they all got older, they even did it with their friends.

When friends came over, we'd play great games with an added twist, which was my favorite part. I'd chase them down and then grab them and toss them into the pool. I'd get some height on the toss so they'd make a big splash when hitting the water. They would then get out and come after me for another round.

For more water fun outside the pool, we added a tub full of super soaker squirt guns for all sorts of water assault games, a tub of water balloons just because we could, and two-lane slip and slides. We were always ready and waiting for some additional sliding fun down our berm. We even had those attachments that sprayed water at you.

To warm up, we had a portable fire pit ready to use or to just sit by at the end of the night. Under our deck, I put up red LED lights around the inside edge, which stayed up year-round, and hung two hammocks. It was truly a great way to relax at night.

Winter Wonderland

When our son was four years old, we got our first portable ice rink. It all came in a kit and was super easy to put together, but it took a long time to build as well as fill. And it kept getting bigger, so the build took even longer. You see, over the years, we had what some boaters call "size envy."

About every three years, the plastic sheet needed to be replaced due to about 300 holes being taped over with super sticky, white, ice rink tape—also part of the kit. So, with each new plastic sheet, I decided to make the rink bigger. The final size was about 40 feet across by 70 feet long, which took up most of our yard, but we definitely made the most of it! The "boards" were made with the snow that I plowed. The more snow we had, the thicker and higher the edges were.

Our berm near the rink had thirteen evergreen trees, and each tree had its own set of single-color, HUGE light bulbs. When on, they truly were a bright and awesome sight to see. We also had two flood lights, one for each edge of the rink, and a portable fire pit (the one we used by the pool in summer) just outside the rink with rubber mats going in a crisscross pattern so the kids could skate off the ice, keep their skates on, and take a break to warm up. Hot cocoa with s'mores were the treat of choice enjoyed with whatever music the group wanted to listen to.

Every year, we tried to do something different with the rink. One year, I thought we could have the kids each paint a scene of their choice somewhere on the ice. I went to the hardware store and bought all kinds of different colored spray paints. We had gold, silver, green, red, blue, yellow, and black. I had each of my kids, Alexa, Tori, and Collin, draw out on paper what they wanted to paint on the ice. The girls did Christmas trees, candy canes, and penguins. Collin had just about every sport represented with soccer, hockey, football, and baseball.

We started out by outlining each design and then filling them in. It took about two to three hours and was a lot of fun. Once it was done, we got back into the house so we could see it better from higher up through the windows. What a marvelous masterpiece our rink was!

Fortunately, there are specific ice rink paints you can buy for such a purpose. Unfortunately, I instead purchased paint with metallic alloys in them, and once the sunlight hit the artwork, the alloys heated up the ice and melted it. This destroyed not only the masterpiece but the ice itself. We had deep grooves in the ice with paint smudges all over. It took about two weeks for me to dilute the alloy mixture enough to recover the rink so the kids could use it again. Live and learn!

As the years went on and lighting technology got better, Collin and I had another AWESOME idea. Let's try putting LED lights in the ice itself and see what happens! We headed to the hardware store. He wanted to have red on both edges and blue along the sides.

Putting up the rink that year took on a new twist. We had to figure out where the first thick layer of ice would come up to on the edges so we could apply the LED lights with super sticky, white tape and then have additional room to add about one more inch of ice on top of them so they wouldn't get cut with skates.

Once the ice was built up, we plugged these strings together to create one continuous strand and then covered the connectors with waterproof tape. In previous years, I had found hockey pucks that actually had a LED lights in them (also blue and red) and we used them on the ice as well. Super cool!

We eventually ended up hosting an annual hockey party in our backyard. (If you're interested in hosting something like that, whether at your home or a nearby rink, I've included some of my party tips in Appendix D.)

News Year's Eve

For years, we also had a New Year's Eve party at our home with our friends and their families. Yet, as our kids got older, they started asking if they could have their friends over, too. Katie and I quickly said that this would be a grand idea.

So, New Year's Eve evolved and became about the kids and their friends. Our Winter Wonderland was ready for them. Inside the house, we had a game room in the basement complete with big screen TV and a potluck buffet in the kitchen.

We knew we had accomplished a safe zone when our daughter Alexa came up during the event and asked if a few of her other friends could come over. It seems that they had gone out to dinner and were not planning on going to any parties after. But they changed their minds and asked if they could come to hers for they knew it was a safe and fun one. Of course the answer was a definite yes.

Then a few of her friends who were already at our house asked if they could go to another party and come back. I asked if their parents knew about this, and they said yes. I requested they call their parents so I could confirm that. I also reminded the kids that if any of the house rules were broken while they were gone, they wouldn't be allowed back into our party that night. I'm happy to say they all came back, and we had more fun and festivities.

Chapter 8
Safety Training

I firmly believe that we need to teach our kids at an early age what to do in emergency situations. The key is to practice them regularly like on the first Saturday of each month.

Fire

When all three kids were very young, I put fire extinguishers throughout the house and showed the kids where they were at: in the kitchen, laundry room, bedroom closets, bathrooms, furnace room, garage, and other rooms. If they needed one anywhere, they would have one.

I also had fold-out ladders in each of the upstairs bedrooms with a solid plate screwed into the wall under the window. We removed the window screen so all they needed to do was put the ladder in its place.

Then, once a month, we would each take a turn showing where the fire extinguishers were on each floor of the house. We would also practice scenarios such as what to do if you are on fire: **stop, drop and roll.** What do you do if you are upstairs and can't get down the stairs? The kids would then show how to pull out the ladders from their closets, put them in place, and open the window. (During practice, they wouldn't open the ladder so it wouldn't damage the outside of the house.) The kids also knew to get away from the house and get to a neighbor's house.

Strangers

Katie and I also talked to them about strangers. As a family, we created a code word that only we would know. If a stranger approached and said Mom and Dad told him to come pick up the kids, the kids would ask for the code word. If the stranger didn't know it, the kids knew to run and scream for help.

If anyone physically picked them up, we encouraged our kids to bite, kick, punch and scream, **"This is not my mother, father, HELP!"**

To practice this, I would literally pick them up in our house and put my hand over their mouths and walk with them. Now, my wife didn't think this was necessary, but we all know that during stressful times, shock sets in and we don't remember what to do. My goal was to get them to fight automatically. Each time I would do this, Katie quickly ran around the house closing all the doors and windows so the neighbors wouldn't worry about what was going on or call the police.

To protect our kids at home in case of a break-in, we had a monitored alarm system, and each floor had an alarm panel. We taught the kids which button to push if someone was trying to break in, which bathroom to go to and how to lock the door. Each bathroom also had a cell phone and the kids knew how to dial 911 as well as what to say and to stay on the line.

As the kids got older and got driver's licenses, we also talked about safety tips for walking to the car when they were by themselves. I told them to keep their keys in-between their fingers with their palms closed around them. They also had mace on their key chains, and I encouraged them to ask someone else to walk them to their car if they felt unsafe or scared.

My goal was to make sure all my kids, both my daughters and my son, knew how to be safe and what to do if they were not. I am happy to say that they have not had to use any of them to date.

The routine practices were noticed. In fact, one of the teachers at a parent–teacher conference said she needed to ask if what she had heard about our safety trainings was true. My wife gave me "the look" and replied, "I must sadly say yes, it is, he does do that on a regular basis." The teacher said that it was great and she wished more parents did it.

So dads, put on your fireman's hat, grab those whistles, place those fire extinguishers, escape ladders, and anything else you see fit to prepare for, and start those drill weekends.

Chapter 9
Mom's Special Treat Plates

When the kids were quite young, they and I conspired to get Mom a very special Christmas present. We thought long and hard but just could not figure out something that would really knock her socks off.

Then, one day, it hit us. As we were driving by, we saw a Paint Your Plate shop and just had to go in and see what it was. To our amazement, it was all kinds of neat blank pottery you could paint any way you wanted.

Well, Tori and Alexa were the only creative ones. Collin and I liked to play sports and video games and had no idea what this painting deal would be like. Yet, we all decided that Mom would really love this.

What to choose for Mom? That was the million dollar question.
Do we each do something for Mom? Or, do we all do one special thing for Mom?

One of them found this BIG serving plate, and we decided that was it! We decided to call it Mom's Special Treats and dated it. And, we figured that since we had put so much effort into it, Mom would want to display treats on it all year round! Or at least display it.

We asked the shopkeeper how to do this project. She gave us a table to ourselves with all of the tools we needed to make it truly our own. We had different types and sizes of paint brushes, water glasses to clean them, so many different colors of paint it was hard to pick, stampers with different designs, and tracing things with all kinds of patterns.

We dove in and figured out what we wanted it to say and added things as we went. The shopkeeper then told us it was a good idea to pencil in ideas and go over them with the paints. So, we began this adventure and what an adventure it was....

Each one of us took a section to make it our own so we could proudly tell Mom what part we did, and yes, even old Dad had a section. We even did the back side of the plate. You can't forget that now, can you? It allowed us to do even more.

We worked like busy little bees and got all the pencilling down and began having one person start painting one section. While that person did that, the rest of us decided to find another piece to paint for fun while we waited our turn.

After four hours, our masterpiece was done! Our ideas had come to life. We told the shopkeeper it was ready to go in the kiln for the final firing.

Not so fast, we found out! She showed us a plate that had one coat of paint versus, two, three, four or more. To make the colors dark and not washed out, we needed to go over everything at least three times.

We needed to come back two more times to finish this? And the other extra "fun" items? She said it would be a great idea, and we could make it an adventure. There was an ice cream store down the block for breaks and many food places as well.

Well, okay then, I said. We would make this our little secret and not tell Mom what we were doing and head out for a day during the next couple of weekends. We went to the ice cream shop and several fun restaurants as well. It became fun and exciting for we could tell that each coating of paint made it look even more AWESOME!

It was finally done and ready for the Kiln. We could not wait to see it after it got fired. Perfectico! Magnificent! And just overall the best treats plate one could have. Boy, we could not wait to give it to Mom and have some yummy treats.

Mom loved it as well and felt it was so special that she did not want to chance it being ruined. So she did not use it for those yummy treats we all had envisioned. It went into a safe hiding place. WHAT?

One would think we would have stopped there but, oh no, we were going to have plates for those treats.

So at the next holiday, Alexa, Tori, Collin and I decided we'd make serving dishes to go along with the treat platter, and eight should do it. That way she would have to let us have some special treats more often than just the holidays, and we would see our hard work as well.

We found the perfect eight, small serving plates. We decided we would each do two and work in a sports theme since Alexa and Tori competitively danced, Collin played hockey, and we all enjoyed watching other sports like baseball, golf and the Olympic games.

We found all kinds of neat stencils and even hand drew some items to make each plate a different sports theme. We knew that this project would take several trips as well, so we figured out all kinds of places we could go to before, during and after our painting adventures like the hamburger malt shop and the ice cream store.

However, even with our planned excursions, the painting soon became a chore, for we had bitten off way too much. Eight plates each needing to be painted three times?

It took us seven trips and twenty-one hours to complete these serving plates for the treats we were going to have, and they turned out just as perfectico and magnificent as the huge serving plate did.

Yet again, Mom felt that they were so special she could not chance them being broken or cracked, especially since she knew which one of us did each plate! So, they hang on the wall for us to see as we walk in and out of the house every single day, and we did not get to enjoy even one treat off of any of the them, including the huge serving plate.

The moral of this story is that things don't always go as planned (as this one seemed to go on forever), yet this can be good. Roll with it, and make it an opportunity to teach your kids and yourself how to adapt and deal with the unexpected. And the process of being on adventures will provide unimaginable "Quality Bonding Time" with each of your kids, something that will be remembered for a lifetime. Finally, you may end up creating something wonderful like keepsakes you can see over the course of your lifetime. In our case, they are up on the wall for us to see and remember every single day!

What will be your next adventure, keepsake or unexpected opportunity to just roll with it?

Chapter 10
Birthdays

Birthdays can be the same old, same old year after year. Of course, not at our home! My wife Katie and I really tried to make birthdays special events that not only our kids and their friends would enjoy, but also our adult friends as well. Here are some of our more memorable events. I hope you'll be able to take some of these ideas and bring them to life for your own children.

Camp Cothoku Island

For Collin's tenth birthday, we created Camp Cothoku Island. It was modeled after the *Survivor* television series and named for our son, Collin Thomas Kubinski.

Since I'm in the printing industry, I had my company's designers make up fake ten dollar and one million dollar bills that had Collin's image, the *Survivor* logo, and the phrase "I Survived Cothoku Island" on them.

Upon arrival, every boy was given camouflage face paint to draw their own unique look for the event. Even good old Dad donned his own look complete with a hunting camouflage outfit. In addition, the boys were given a preparation kit filled with: a bag, camo head band, Cyclone water bottle, Rice Krispies bar, Nutri-Grain bar, gummy worms, cookies, trail mix, beef jerky, Twizzlers, and more. [In the interest of safety and fun, no peanut items were prepared or included, so it didn't contaminate the competition equipment. EpiPens were present at all times, just in case.]

Each participant drew for a colored bandana to see which team they would be on. We did teams and not individual competition to bring them together. We also let them know that arguing or being negative (including tattling) would result in sitting out a round. Then we laid out the ground rules and pointed out the "No Hunting" sign at the perimeter which informed them they had now entered the survivor island area.

Each "contestant" was given his own tiki torch that was lit, and they carried into the area. After they were all inside the make shift arena in the backyard, we extinguished them and then relit them at the end of the event.

We took hunting gear, outdoor blind materials, Camel backpacks filled with soft weights and a variety of our swing set materials to make up an obstacle course. The path was spray painted on the grass so they knew exactly where to go. Each teammate would put on one of the weighted backpacks, run through the course and return to base camp to give the next teammate the pack while the other team ran the course.

While either wearing or carrying the pack, each "survivor" had to get through the tire swing, up the swing set ladder, around the hunting blinds, across the jungle gym, over the slide obstacle, crawl down and through the hidden crawl space and back to base camp. The team with the fastest time won.

The second competition had the kids shooting an air gun at a target while sitting behind the hunting blind. Each shooter wore eye protection, and kids chose a variety of stances from which to shoot. The team with the highest total score won. [I would recommend setting up two stations to keep it moving along. This took some time.] Many had not shot a gun or pistol before, and we showed them how to shoot the air gun. You could see a lot of happy faces during the event, as well as some anticipation.

Archery was next on the list. The archery range began at the top of the swing set platform which was hidden behind outdoor camouflage. Here we had an actual bow and arrows with blunted ends, and we placed a variety of targets at different distances. Again, this was a first time experience for many of the kids, so we gave some assistance. Helping them do it for the first time and seeing their expressions as they released their first arrow and hit the mark was the best.

Each target had its own point system based on distance and size of the target which were things like fake deer and crows. [Yes, we had adult supervision if you count me, for I am sometimes considered my wife's fourth child.] And the team with the most points won.

For our fourth event, kids cast a fishing line into our portable pool and tried to snag different size rings. Points for each ring size was added up for a grand total.

While we had planned a diving event where competitors were "blindfolded" by painted eye goggles, we ran out of time.

We restored our energy reserves on *Survivor*-themed cake, hot dogs, chips, and energy drink before popping corn over the outdoor fire.

At the end, it was dark, and the boys were spent. Who are we kidding? Dad and the helpers were spent. The boys were raring to continue. We relit each tiki torch and walked back to the front of the house while chanting, "Camp Cothoku, we survived Camp Cothoku; Camp Cothoku, we survived Camp Cothoku." Once there, each team was lined up, one on each side of the driveway, with their lit tiki torches.

You can imagine what the parents were thinking as they pulled up to the house in the dark with this site and the chanting. They didn't know what had occurred but knew the boys had had a great time.

The torches were extinguished, and each kid received an official certificate of participation that I got from the Minnesota Department of Natural Resources which had their name on it and was signed by the person in charge of Mentoring Program Coordination. It stated, "This Certificate is awarded to [name of kid], Certificate of Participation. This certificate entitles the youth all the positive experiences the outdoors has to offer. Minnesota Dpt. Of Natural Resources." I even received fishing lures that were blank with materials to decorate and color them, but we ran out of time to do that as well.

If parents wanted, instead of going home right away, they could stay awhile and enjoy the outdoor fireplace, food and drink, and watch the kids go through the competitions again. It was truly a blast!

No Rules

Every year for awhile, my son, about eight to ten of his buddies, one other dad and myself would head up north to my in-laws cabin for a weekend of **NO Rules, NO Girls, NO Moms** while staying up late, sleeping in and eating anything our hearts desired while we played, played, played. Did I say play?

Here's a portion of the invite that went out. For the parents that did not know me or my humor yet, this was their first taste of it all.

You're invited to Collin's Annual B-Day Party

Date: 9-7 until 9-9

RSVP as soon as you can due to short notice

Return Home on 9-9. Depending on weather and how much fun the boys are having, we might stay a bit longer. Will have boys call you when we leave, which should take about two hours to get home once we leave.

Dear parents and especially moms,

By dropping your son off, you are opting in, and here is the risk you are taking by leaving your son with me:

Rules; there are NO rules.

- Nothing but junk food will be eaten.

- No sleep times set.

- No supervision will be done, I may or may not be present where they are, but probably not. I'll be sleeping or other things that intrigue me.

- They will come back, but not sure what shape they will be in when you pick them up Sunday.

- We have not lost anyone yet, but there is always a first time.

- We have not had any injuries yet, but again, there is always a first time.

- TOUGH love is the only type of affection/discipline/supervision that will be shown. Believe me, it is TOUGH!

- NO moms can come up or show up at all. This is the only RULE in place. I guess I lied about the rules. Ha ha.

So, if you can abide by all of the above, please drop off your son. If he doesn't show up, I'll know you did not trust the supervision. But hey, who could blame you.

Also, dads, you cannot come up either for I can only watch and manage myself. Even though this may sound like heaven to you and it is, you cannot show up either. Ha, ha!

As part of the invite, we included a complete list of the food items needed for the two days as well as a sign-up sheet for who would bring what like 48 eggs, two gallons of milk and grapes, blueberries and spaghetti squash. (Okay, I guess it wasn't all junk food. I guess I lied again.) I also added a what-to-pack list which included a swim suit, toiletries, and "money for arcade games and poker nights—I need the easy money, so give them lots." The sort-of planned events included swimming, hot tubbing, tubing, jet skiing, a variety of sports competitions like kickball and tennis, air hockey, water balloon fights and anything else we could squeeze in before the weekend was over. I relented a little by including a tentative menu for each day and a list of the other attendees, which included the boys and two adult chaperones. Well, okay, we invited the boys to watch us and not us them.

I am proud to say, that every year it was AWESOME for not only the boys, but the other dad and myself. We enjoyed them, made sure they were safe, had fun, cleaned up and were respectful. But don't let any of the parents know this for it will ruin my reputation.

Camping, Fishing and Hunting Adventure

This birthday, I tried to come up with something that was truly unique and different that many of the boys hadn't done. With our back yard being a perfect setting to have all of the stations and events put up, we made it happen and was a HUGE success!

So be creative! Work with what you have! And enjoy the process.

Chapter 11
The Best Christmas Ever
—for Collin

You already know about the Winter Wonderland and our AWESOME ice rink. Well, this one Christmas, all Collin wanted was a good goalie net with a goalie blocker mat so he could practice shooting.

I headed to a sports consignment shop and found a regulation goal and brought it to the house days before Christmas so he wouldn't see it.

I then went online and found a GREAT plastic formed goalie blocker and a bucket of 100 hockey pucks. It all showed up just in time for me to put the goalie blocker on the net and place it on the ice Christmas Eve. The bucket of pucks was sitting underneath the deck.

Christmas Day came and all the kids opened their gifts. The girls loved theirs because they got what they wanted. Yet, Collin just didn't seem to be enjoying the little knick-knacks we got him; they missed the mark entirely. However, he handled it like a champ.

When all the gifts had been opened and Katie was going to start making breakfast, I asked Collin if we should head out onto the rink and shoot a little bit while Mom made breakfast. He was all for that. It took what seemed like forever for Collin to get his gear on.

As he got to the deck and looked out onto the ice, he stopped dead in his tracks. He looked at the rink, then at me and then back to the rink about three or four times. Finally, the BIGGEST smile came across his face and "This is the BEST Christmas ever!" was heard across the yard.

He ran down the stairs and got out on the ice without his stick or a puck to see the goal and goalie blocker. I went underneath the deck, got his stick and the bucket of pucks, and once again, "This is the BEST Christmas ever!" was heard.

What neither my wife nor I realized was that this blue, pre-fabbed goalie blocker was so strong, that every one of Collin's hits on the blocker sounded like a gun shot. And he had 100 shots on goal before he had to take a break. This was okay during the day, but he was out there most nights as well, especially with the Winter Wonderland lights and fire pit. When his friends came over, they all lined up on the ice, and it was like a shooting gallery.

Our poor neighbors. But it was indeed the "BEST Christmas ever!" for Collin.

Chapter 12
The Room Under the Stairs

Our first two children were girls, and boy, did they love their Barbies. We had a countless number of dolls, clothes, accessories, houses, cars, baskets, rockers, and more. Every time I came downstairs, the area was overflowing with Barbie merchandise.

However, underneath our stairs was an unfinished storage area complete with door that we used as our tornado safety zone. Why not finish it off with carpet and lights for the girls so they would have somewhere to put all those wonderful Barbie doll items? So we did just that. It was wonderful, and they really enjoyed this special area that was their own.

As they grew up and the Barbies were no longer of interest, we let it become our safety area once again with pillows, blankets, flashlights, and extra batteries.

However, I had another great idea. (They just come to me sometimes.) Why not let the kids paint it any way they wanted and have their friends sign it and personalize it with hand prints? So they did. They put plastic over the carpet and painted it a bright, almost neon yellow and then splatter-painted blues, oranges, and greens all around. It looked great.

We then put permanent markers of all sizes amongst the emergency stuff so they could put up drawings, nicknames, quotes, or hand prints. The only rule was that the additions must meet with my approval, and if anyone did something questionable, we'd have a talk, and they would fix it.

It was a huge SUCCESS, and many participated. In fact, we even had two Japanese foreign exchange students we invited to participate. Yet, their culture did not allow them to ruin anything. It took a lot of encouragement from me for them to do it. I even put the paint on their hands and placed them on the wall. After that was done, I handed them permanent markers and showed them what others had done. I then told them they could write anything they wanted. After some misgivings, they gave in with gusto and covered one-quarter of the wall! It took awhile for us to get what they wrote translated, but they left each of us a personal note and one to our whole family which read:

"I am so happy to know this family, and I did not want to come back to Japan. I don't know when, but I am going to come back and see them again. I will study English hard so I can communicate with them. I am just writing what is in my mind, but I know someone will translate this and understand what I am saying. I don't trust many people but I felt so safe with this family. I love this family and I will never forget them."

It is so COOL seeing the unique Japanese characters there.

Every home should have a special room like this one for their kids and their friends!

Chapter 13
Dad's Rights and Duties as It Relates to Dating

I perceive a father has particular duties as it relates to dating and his children, especially his daughters. There are two I'd like to highlight.

One: It is my God-given right, duty and privilege to put the FEAR of God into each and every boy who wishes to date my daughters. You can't ever take that away from me!

Two: It is my right and privilege to embarrass my children as much as possible.

I must say, I enjoy fulfilling these rights and duties and definitely consider it a privilege. I also consider it full circle as many of us men experienced this from the other side as we dated other dads' daughters. Didn't they try to put the fear of GOD into us so we didn't step over any lines? I figure it's my turn!

First and foremost is the application to date my daughter. There are many of these out on the internet from which to choose, and I highly recommend printing one out and copying it many times to use as a threat to your daughters and each prospective boy during their dating time. It has many fantastic questions that I have used as well.

A few of my favorite questions include:

- Do you own a van, truck with oversize tires, waterbed or pickup truck with a mattress in the back?

- In fifty words or less, what does LATE mean to you?

- In fifty words or less, what does "DON'T TOUCH MY DAUGHTER" mean to you?

- Which church do you attend and how often?

- When is the best time for me to interview your [parents, priest, minister or rabbi]?

- The last place on your body that you would want to have shot would be:

- If beaten, the last bone I would want broken would be:

- The one thing I hope this application doesn't ask me about is:

- [And this is the BEST one!] At the bottom of the application: "Please allow six years for processing."

As reinforcement, I picked up a great sign at the Minnesota State Fair. It sits in my den right next to my gun cabinet, which has a very nice selection by the way. It states:

> **Yes, I do have a beautiful daughter...**
>
> **I also have a GUN, a shovel and an alibi!**

It's easy to take a photo of it and email it to my kids, too—as a reminder, of course.

It was when our oldest daughter was about fourteen or so and going on a group date that I first attempted to meet "the boyfriend" and have a dating "talk," but to no avail.

According to her, this was really not dating. They were just a bunch of friends getting together and doing things. I asked a couple questions to clarify:

- How many are going? She said about fourteen.

- How many are boys? She said seven.

- I said, "If there is one boy per girl, then you are on a date, and I should be able to do my duty as father and meet him and have the talk."

I was met with a resounding NO, along with the whole "it's not a date" thing again.

I relented until another dad called and told me the group was seeing a movie near my home. He also told me when and which movie.

At the appropriate time, I left my office about 45 minutes away from home, drove to the movie theater, bought a large pop and popcorn with all the fixings, and proceeded to sit in the front row, in the first seat on the left end so when they came in, they would see me.

I heard them coming; they were all excited about the movie. One by one, they walked by. After about ten of them had passed, Alexa finally noticed me. I did not say a word but simply gave her the signal that said, "I've got my eyes on you" and then turned my head toward the screen.

Her look of utter shock, disbelief, concern and who knows what else was priceless. As she went to sit with the rest of them halfway back, I heard her whisper, "That's my dad, and he is right there in front. We need to move."

I watched the whole movie and left when the credits came up. I drove home and did not say a word to my wife. However, when Alexa got home, she immediately went to Katie and regaled the saga.

Both of them came to me in the den and gave me "the look." I simply stated that I had had a bad day at work and needed to unwind. "How would I know that you all were going to be there?" I asked, and then added, "But, why not let me meet him and have the talk?"

Alexa responded, **"NOOOOOOO!"**

I said, "Okay, but it will have to happen sooner or later."

"I said we are not dating," Alexa said.

My wife backed Alexa up by adding, in my direction, "That will not be happening."

So, I let it sit.

Wouldn't you know, my buddy called me again about two weeks later and said they were going again. I asked for the movie and time. Again, I got in the car, drove to the theater, ordered a large pop and popcorn with all the fixings, and proceeded to the front row, first seat and waited.

The entire scenario repeated itself down to the "I've got my eye on you" signal and my daughter's horrified whisper about needing to move seats.

Once my daughter got home, I was again confronted by both my wife and daughter. Once again, I calmly stated that I had had a bad day and had gone to a movie, and wouldn't it be a good time for me to meet him since these things seem to be happening for a reason? I also hinted to my daughter that she should be on her best behavior because, as she was discovering, I am everywhere.

Three Different Types of Talks

Talk One is for group dating. There is no real talk here with the boy; it's just a warning to your daughter that The Talk is coming. This part of The Talk is when we give expectations to the daughter on what to look for in a boy and get her thinking about how she wants to be treated, talked to and respected—have her make decisions on what behaviors by the boy are acceptable or not.

Talk Two is when the daughter plans to go on a date one-on-one. Mom, Dad, Daughter and The Date are all present. Usually, this is when the females glare at Dad with the look that says, "You'd better not scare him off!" It's a very different talk than the one-on-one Dad has alone with the boy.

Talk Two usually goes something like this:

"[The Date], let me tell you what dating means to me. There are two different types of dates. One is where you are looking for the person you will spend the rest of your life with. There are many things you go through on those dates to see if the other person complements you and completes you. That's not where you are now."

"This second type of date is where you're at. You and Daughter are discovering what it is to date—how to act and treat each other with respect, both privately and publicly."

"For instance, how do you treat her at school. Are you too cool to acknowledge her with more than a "Hey, wassup?" Or do you respect her and say something appropriate? What about PDA (public displays of affection)? For you, in my mind, acceptable behaviors include: handholding. That's it. Short list."

"Yet, there is a lot more to that. I have given my daughters the tools they need to help them out of situations, and your role or job is to not put them in those situations where they need to use those tools. Basically, [The Date], your job is to be me while you are with my daughter, and I need to ask you [as I look straight in his eyes], **can I trust you to be me when you are with my daughter?"**

You can only imagine what response you get not only from the boy but also your daughter and your wife! It's not a pretty sight, but it sure sends a message and is quite funny at the same time. Disclaimer: yes, you'll have some digging out to do with your daughter and the number of times you'll have to say sorry to your wife for this may be unlimited. But, hey! It's my right, duty and privilege!

Talk Three comes when you can get The Date alone and in the Man Cave, as I call my little sanctuary, and is only used on those that you feel need the extra authority and scare tactic. We all know that there may be times where this tactic will be used and this is open for interpretation and changes as you see fit.

My man cave has a very nice glass-paned gun cabinet filled with a variety of weaponry: shot guns, rifles, hand guns, a compound bow, survival knives and martial arts nunchucks. This is where the "Gun, Shovel and Alibi" sign hangs. As we enter, I may also drop hints about my being a third gup in Tae Kwon Do, which is just two belts away from black belt, and I've done many full-contact competitions and caused a few broken bones.

Once in the man cave, I sit in my high-back chair conveniently located in front of the gun cabinet. On my desk, there just happens to be my Glock 45 hand gun being cleaned. The Date gets to sit in a nearby, low-setting chair looking up at me.

So, the stage has been set and we begin to have whatever type of talk we need to be having. But, the gist of the talk is that I am very protective of my daughters and family and am a very good shot with my handgun, which, I pick up (unloaded, of course) and hand to him. As he is holding it, looking at it, feeling the weight of it in his hands, I invite him to go to a shooting range with me—so he can see what a good shot I am.

Actually, Talk Three has never happened. I've rehearsed it. Memorized it. Would have had fun delivering it. And it's a talk for which every father should be prepared. But I've never had to actually use it. However, all my daughters' dates have been in my man cave and seen the gun cabinet. I imagine they understand what it's all about.

The Talk Rumors Spread

Rumors about my guns and the talk I'd like to give have spread. But I ask: is that a bad thing?

Our house has always been known to be a safe place with no tolerance for any drinking or drugs. I stress this at each event as I am a recovering alcoholic. When any boys come over, I always greet each one with a handshake to let them know I am home, and I reaffirm that there is no drinking or drugs at our home.

Just before Alexa's senior year in high school, she had a co-ed party in our backyard playland. Since it was summer, both my wife and I were at work when it started. I came home and saw everyone enjoying themselves: kids in the pool, kids on the hammocks.

As I walked out quietly, I heard a girl telling the story about the guns in my cabinet and my sign. And it was not my daughter. As I walked down the deck stairs, she said, "There he is," as she saw my shoes coming down the steps and quickly stopped telling the story.

I went out and greeted all the boys not under the deck with a hello and handshake and then proceeded to those sitting on the hammocks. There were about five people on each hammock and, as I went to each boy, one piped up and said, "Mr. Kubinski, is it true you have a gun collection?"

I swooshed the girl sitting next to him aside to make room for myself and sat down right next to him, put my arm around his shoulders, and said, "Why yes, it is true I have a very nice gun collection. Do you and I need to have the gun talk?"

He said, "Ah, nooooo."

It is great to know that your reputation precedes you.

However, at dinner that night, the females in my home were horrified that this story was being repeated and that I was getting this reputation. I let them talk and get it all out, and then I piped up.

"You know, I was a high school boy once, and let me tell you, there are two different types of dates that can occur. The first is where the boy simply drives up in his car, sits in the driveway, honks his horn for the girl to come out, and leaves without ever having to deal with the parents. That's a date where a lot of bad things can happen and that type will not occur here."

"The second is where the boy knows full well that he will be dealing with a dad like me each and every time he picks you up. Now, he is either a manipulator and troublemaker like Eddie Haskell or he truly likes you and is willing to go through whatever it takes. Just think of all the bad dates I'm saving you from!"

None of the women felt my philosophy was sound. However, it is my God-given right, duty and privilege to put the fear of God into each and every boy who wishes to date my daughters. That's my story and I'm sticking to it!

Marine Card

Whenever I am out at lunch and see men or women in military uniform, I try to buy their meals anonymously and have the cashier tell them, "Thanks for your service and the sacrifices you and your family make for us to enjoy the liberties that we have. Have a great day."

One day, I was in line at Chipotle with some colleagues. I noted a Marine in his dress blues, so I walked up to the cashier, said I'd like to pay for his meal anonymously, and asked her to thank him for his service and sacrifice.

I then took my place back in line and waited for my turn to order.

Sometime during our lunch, the Marine came up to our table, handed me his business card, and thanked me for buying his lunch. He added, "Let me know if there is anything the Marines can do for you!"

Now, being the loud and obnoxious father that I am, and given my duty to watch over my daughters, as well as embarrass them as much as possible, I had an A-ha! moment. I said to him, "Well, I'd love it if you would call my daughter's boyfriend. You could introduce yourself, let him know you're acquainted with me, and that I thought he'd be a prime candidate for the Corps! Then ask him when a good time to swing by would be!"

We all laughed, but I knew full well this would not go over well if I actually had him do it, but I kept the card.

At dinner that night, our entire family was gathered and enjoying the meal: me, my wife Katie, Alexa, Tori and Collin. I pulled out the Marine's card and handed it to Alexa and mentioned he'd be calling The Date tomorrow.

You could only imagine the looks I got from around the table. My son Collin loved it and found it to be extremely funny as did I. Yet, for some reason the females of the household did not. I had to assure them that this was not actually being done, but it sure was an awesome idea, don't you think?

Chapter 14
Standing Out in the Crowd

Remember how I said it is my right and privilege to embarrass my children as much as possible? Well, you're about to see it in full motion.

Benilde-St. Margaret's High School has 26 varsity sports and is known as the Red Knights. Not surprisingly, their team colors are red and white.

Both of my daughters attended BSM and both made it to state for dance. The first time I attended the state tournament, it was at Target Center in downtown Minneapolis.

The idea is to get to the tournament early and get the best possible seats you can for the whole parent and cheering section so that the girls can look out in the middle and see a sea of red cheering them on. Well, we did get the best section, front and center, and there was a sea of red cheering them on.

But that sea didn't include their good old dad. Nope. I was wearing the brightest neon green shirt I had and you could see me a mile away amongst all that crimson. Not only was I not conforming to the way things have always been—tradition—but my shirt color was similar to a competitor's school colors as well, and they were in the stands next to us.

How did I discover my social misstep? Not only did my wife and every other BSM parents look at me in disbelief as I took my coat off to sit with them, but they also rolled their eyes and said a few things under their breath. My wife immediately told me that this was definitely cause for a discussion some other time.

After the event, Alexa said, "Dad, I can't believe you did that! My head coach pulled me aside and asked me if that was my dad wearing the neon green in the sea of red. I looked down and shook my head and sadly said, 'Yes, it is' and walked away."

I then asked Alexa within my wife's hearing, "Alexa, did you know that I was there?" I paused a moment. "Will you remember that I was there?"

She said yes.

"Well then, you should be overjoyed! If I was to have worn red like everyone else, you would never have known for sure if I was there or where I was sitting," I said. "But you know plain and simple that I was indeed there cheering you on and exactly where I was sitting. In fact, everyone on your team including your coaches knew I was there cheering all of you on. You'll remember this for the rest of your life. So, don't you think that is awesome?"

I guess she didn't see it that way at the time, but eventually, she and I have had a few good laughs about it. She still can't believe I did it, but she admits that she knows I was there as does everyone else.

Bet you're saying to yourself, he won't be making that same mistake again! Will he?

Oops, I did it again.

My son Collin attended Wayzata High School, team colors navy blue, gold and white. So the cheering section is a sea of blue, and I wore a red winter jacket and hat to all of his high school hockey games until his senior year when my wife bought me a black jacket and told me I wasn't allowed to wear the red one anymore.

Ironically, the first day I wore the black coat to a hockey game, a few parents came up to me on my way out and said, "Oh, you are here. We looked all over for you in your red coat and didn't see you."

Moral of the story? Stand out any way you can for your kids' sake, even if your wife isn't completely on board!

Chapter 15

Not Under the Influence

Discussing drugs and alcohol with your kids can be uncomfortable.
When do you have the talk and what do you say in hopes of getting
through and making a point that is remembered?

Well, I have to admit that this is trial and error for everyone. There is
no perfect talk, no perfect time. However, I have more experience than
most. As of this printing, I am blessed to be a recovering alcoholic of
more than sixteen years and am in Alcoholics Anonymous.

Drawing on some of the many tools available within this program and
in talking with others in recovery and their families, I came up with the
following and hope it helps you.

I sat each one of our children down in my man cave at a time that I felt
was appropriate for them. I told them, "I'm not naive. I know that I can't
stop you from drinking or doing drugs. Yet, I can give you the facts and
life lessons that I have lived through and experienced in hopes that you
too learn from them before getting into trouble yourself or having and
have to experience similar negatives in your lifetime."

I asked my kids to ask themselves "why" if and when they chose to drink
or use drugs. Was it because they really liked the taste or effect it offered
up? Was it because they felt they needed to escape from something? Was
it peer pressure, "everybody else is doing it?" Or perhaps they wanted
one at this time with no intent to get drunk or high?

"How you answer each one of those at the time you are about to partake should tell you something. I hope that your mother and I have instilled in you a positive and strong self-image so that you don't feel you need to do any of this to conform to others, or use it to run away from things. Instead, tackle those items head-on without drugs and alcohol."

"Yet, if it simply is a casual drink, and you are of age, then it is what it was meant to be."

"If you are under age and drinking, then we need to talk it out and figure out things so you don't get in trouble, hurt others or yourself. Again, I don't accept it, but I can't necessarily stop it from happening. No one wants their kids to hide or sneak it or put themselves or others in dangerous situations. So, talking about it, being honest and trying to figure out options is all you can do."

"If it is drugs, then we really need to address things on all fronts."

"Our home is a safe and fun place for you and your friends. Both your mother and I want you to feel comfortable about talking openly to us about anything. We will NOT condemn, punish or make you feel sorry for coming to us to talk about any of this at any time. Nor will we ask questions, punish you or make you feel sorry or uncomfortable if you call us when someplace else and need us to come pick you up to get away from it. So, please just come to talk to us or call us any time of day or night."

I am happy to say that all three of them have at one time or another called us to pick them up to get away from a compromising situation or have come to talk to us about things going on and how they are feeling.

So, I hope this helps you with your kids in making the right choices at the right times and for the right reasons.

If you have concerns, keep in mind there are groups and resources out there I would recommend. Three of them are:

Alcoholics Anonymous (AA). If you are concerned about a drinking problem, you can find more information and help at aa.org.

Al-Anon is for friends and family members of problem drinkers. For more information on that group, go to al-anon.alateen.org.

Teen-Anon is for teens with alcohol or drug abuse issues and those who love them. You can find more resources at teen-anon.com/addict.htm.

Chapter 16
Family Vacations

The Dude Ranch

If you want to take a vacation that will be different, fun and provide you and your kids memories for a lifetime, then consider a dude ranch. This is something that you need to experience for yourself in its truest form!

My wife found one outside of Jackson Hole in Kelly, Wyoming. We booked it for early July and then prepped for it; we bought cowboy boots, dude hats, bandanas, jean jackets, leather gloves and a bunch of other stuff they let us know we needed. We were prepared, ready and willing.

We then flew out for our two weeks of firsts! Our kids were 15, 13 and 9 at the time. I won't tell you how old I and my wife were.

We first stayed at Jackson Lake Resort in Lake Jackson, Wyoming, and had a breakfast of reindeer waffles while overlooking the beautiful Teton Mountains.

We then meandered our way through two days at Yellowstone National Park. We were privileged to see the rushing water rapids on one side of the park and the timberlines on the other. The whole drive had such breathtaking scenery.

We got to the Continental Divide and saw Old Faithful. I had no idea! I had heard all about it, but it was awesome in person. The hot springs were smelly but also quite a sight. And buffalo. They walked in front, in back and right next to our car. We could have rolled down our windows and touched them. They are HUGE and magnificent animals. There were so many must-take photo moments.

That night, we stopped in Gardiner, Montana, at a quaint little Italian restaurant and then went to bed early. On our way back through the park, we made a snowman alongside the road at an elevation of about 8,500 feet in our shorts and sandals. As we took pictures of us next to our creation, others came and took their photos with our snowman.

We then stopped along the lake, had a picnic lunch, and visited the Jackson Wildlife Art Museum

That night, our hotel wasn't quite what I had imagined it would be, so we kept going until we came to The Rustic Inn which had only been open two weeks. And we got to enjoy the Fourth of July fireworks from their pool. How COOL is that!

Jackson Hole has a lot of sightseeing and touristy things to do. A few we chose to do included visiting the Ripley's Believe It or Not museum, seeing an old-time movie theater, and walking down a ski slope.

The next day we whitewater rafted down the Snake River. The river was high and fast. We donned our safety helmets, life jackets, and wet suits. The water was cold, but we didn't care. We even hit a level four rapids and went up and down like the champs we were. The company we picked had one of the highest safety ratings and had a guy in a small kayak going both ahead to check things out and behind to make sure all were safe not only in our group but the many other groups following.

On July 7, we took a one-hour drive to our final destination: The Red Rock Ranch. Holy schnikey. What a breathtaking view! Apparently, we got lucky our first try because others there, who had traveled the world and experienced other dude ranches, said the help at Red Rock stay in better places than the guests at others.

We stayed in the cabin named Apache which was in the heart of the ranch. We had a week filled with games, new friends, food and picturesque views. The kids had their own kids-only building, and the adults had their own bar and game room, too.

For outdoor sports, pickleball was the game of choice. It's kind of a combination of tennis, badminton, and ping pong. Professional fly fishermen also came in and taught us how to fly fish at one of the many deep ponds they had filled with trout. And we enjoyed a square dance one night as well as a cowboy poet and fiddler.

Being that it was a dude ranch, each person was outfitted with a horse according to his or her riding abilities, which really made the difference. You were responsible for the horse's care during and after each ride. Brushing out and bonding became a natural thing to do.

My horse was called Lucy Lui, but I quickly renamed her Super Sneaky Snacker Lucy Lui for she found every chance possible to bend down and sneak something to eat both while idling or trailblazing. Katie had Sage, Alexa had Slue Foot, Tori had Blue Miner, and Collin rode Moses whom we called the fart master. No one wanted to ride behind him.

Each day, the kids and adults had their own trail riding time. We could also go out as a family or as a couple any time we wanted. A vacation within a vacation.

On one of our rides, Katie and I chose to go up to the skyline from 7,200 feet to 9,300 feet above sea level. It was a gorgeous sight as we enjoyed our picnic lunch with our feet overhanging the cliff and viewing the Tetons way in the background.

On two occasions, we had breakfast rides. The first was complete with pancakes, scrambled eggs, bacon and good old campfire coffee and hot cocoa for the kids. Lake Grizzly was another family ride where we packed up breakfast and took it with us. We rode through streams, steep terrain and beautiful flower fields to the lake. We enjoyed the picnic meal and then went in for a COLD swim in the lake. Of course, I was first to go in and had to tell everyone how warm it was while they hesitated for what seemed to be hours before finally jumping in and finding out just how cold it was. Yet, since they were in, we made the best of it and of course another photo-tunistic moment.

Wagon BBQ kids' ride was one night for them while the parents had an elegant meal. They really enjoyed this time with their new friends as we did ours. I ended up in the kitchen with their head chef, also named Tom, where I made for him, the staff and our friends, my uncle's (or "Unkster") famous Creole shrimp dish. It gets hotter the longer it sits in the sauce, and you dip preferably freshly-made bread into it.

"Let the Games Begin" was a show at the end of the week where the kids performed horse-riding tricks they had learned such as a donut-eating contest, "no hands" while on horseback, and wheel barrow races.

A contest between kids and adults was also held to see who could drive the cattle best. Once you heard your cow's number called, you needed to drive the cattle, thin out the one whose number was called and get it into the pen. The kids beat the adults handily.

The final dinner was a family BBQ to which we rode. The meal was incredible and the kids received special horseshoe awards. For Alexa, it was great attitude. For Tori, most talented, and for Collin, The Natural.

As mementos, you could brand the Red Rock Ranch logo onto anything. So we did our hats, gloves, boots, and jeans. Here is where we took our Christmas card picture, too, while sitting next to rushing water. Truly a memory of a lifetime captured!

After a great stay, it was time to take all those last-minute pictures with all our new friends, get phone numbers and addresses to stay in touch and of course, buy the Red Rock Ranch memory book they have.

Best of all, they gave us about 150 pictures on a disc of moments they had captured for all of us during the trip to add to our own photos.

On our plane ride home, Katie, who is 100 percent responsible for making this incredible trip happen, put together a photo album and sent it to Shutterfly for us to have as a keepsake that we always have on display in our home.

"Well done, Katie," I said. "I love you and am a very lucky man!"

Cruises

On a cruise, you can visit many different places without ever having to pack, move, and unpack. Plus, you have so many options of things to do for both parents and kids if planned correctly. My wife and I have been on three cruises: two by ourselves and one with our whole family.

When we book cruises, we typically use Royal Caribbean Princess Cruises. The ship size is just right and you don't feel like you're crammed into a sardine can. But each year, new ships come out for you to consider. We typically reserve a cabin with a balcony so we can sit outside our room and relax while listening to the ocean. It's also a great spot to have dinner delivered.

When selecting our room, we usually choose the outside cabins mid-ship because they seem to be less rocky. And we get a cabin window which helps avoid a feeling of confinement. Word to the wise: make sure you don't have a lifeboat blocking your view. We also avoid being too near elevators and stairs, and we make sure we're not above or below discos or propellers!

Seven days and about four stops seemed to be just perfect for us. We had time to cruise and experience the many activities on board with a few ports where we could go exploring. When we booked our cruise, we also booked the excursions we felt sure we wanted to do. For others, we figured it out as the excursion got closer. We have enjoyed: ziplining, horseback riding on the beach, tubing down the river, walking up waterfalls, snorkeling, scuba diving, catamaran sailing, swimming with dolphins, duty-free shopping, and riding in both helicopters and submarines!

Camping

Camping: what a great way to spend some quality time as a family! You're unplugged and really getting to know and bond with your kids.

Our first year, we used a tent. Now we "glamp," or glamour camp, by renting a pop-up trailer which has a lot of the comforts of home!

Over the years, I've learned the hard, or expensive, way that I need to take notes on what to bring each year, or I end up replacing the items again while we are on the trip. So, at the back of the book is a fairly thorough what-to-bring list if you're considering this adventure as your next family outing!

Chapter 17
Father and Son Bonding Time

Three good friends of mine and Katie's have played hockey all their lives. They played in high school, got some ice time in college and even now are in what's called an old timers' league. They are all great skaters, truly know the game, and LOVE it. Their boys love it as well.

They also know that I was a competitive swimmer. You know, liquid water, not this frozen stuff. And they know that I never learned how to skate. Swim team season was during hockey season. They know I love watching hockey, both college and professional, and that I am tickled pink that my son has picked it up. How could he not when all of his cousins play and my wife talked me into buying a hockey rink kit to put up on our backyard since he was four?

When they came to me and said, "Tom, how would you like to go with us to a summer hockey camp for five days with your son and stay in a dorm-like setting and watch him really learn the art of hockey?" I said, "Sign me up; I'd love to do this with my son." Since I never got to do this with my father, it was something that I truly wanted to experience with my son, Collin. So, we signed up, and that's when it all started to get a little bit odd.

The bill came and, quite honestly, it seemed quite high for what I thought we were paying for—a dorm room with dorm beds, no air conditioning, cafeteria-type food and hockey practice ice time. Yet, I didn't pay it any real mind and sent in the payment.

About two weeks after I paid the bill, Scott, one of the three dads came up to me and said, "Tom, we forgot to tell you that on the last day, the fathers play hockey against their sons. You will need to get some gear." What a great idea! I figured I'd just borrow my brother-in-law's gear, buy some used skates and a stick and be all over that. It will be a good to time to watch, participate and let them have fun at my expense, I thought. So I splurged on a $20 pair of skates and a stick.

After another two weeks goes by, Andy, another one of the three guys approaches me and says, "Tom, we forgot to tell you that the dads play a game against the dads. But don't worry, it's like real hockey; they have lines of talent, and you should be in the line with similar dads." I said, "What, you are kidding me, right?" How many dads with kids this age will come to this and not be able to skate? I doubt more than a few, and there are five on each line of each side. There would have to be ten guys who couldn't skate for me to be "in line" with them. That's when I got serious and bought new gear.

Mark, the third and final dad, came up to me two weeks later and said, "Tom, we forgot to tell you, the kids practice two times a day for about one or two hours each time, and the dads are on the ice with them for each one as well. Plus the dads play a dads' game each night." I said, "Okay now. You all invited me just to have a good laugh at me since I don't know how to skate." He said, "That pretty much sums it up, but you'll have an awesome time."

So, my packing list included an extra-large quantity of ice packs, HUGE bottles of aspirin and Aleve besides everything else I had planned. Oh, and Febreze.

Hockey camp time finally came, and we arrived at camp and got in line to check in. The head coach for camp also coached a farm team for pros. We were in his line. When I got up there, I said, "Coach, I was really excited about coming down with my son, Collin, to see what a hockey camp was all about and to watch him learn and improve, not to mention all of the father and son bonding time we were going to experience. Yet, I need to tell you that all of that is now null and void."

Coach, and all the other dads and kids, especially Collin, were sitting there wondering where I was going with this. "Troy, you see, I was invited here under false pretenses," I said. "I had no idea being able to skate as a father and participant on the ice was in the mix. For you see, I have NO idea how to skate; I was a competitive swimmer. So, Troy, it has now become what you and your staff can teach me during our time here and not what you can do for Collin."

Everyone laughed. Troy told me that his staff would do a great job with Collin and that there was hope for me.

We got into our rooms and unpacked. On our door were signs with our names and a star for every year we'd been at camp. So that would be exactly one. The other guys all had two or three on theirs.

We then went to check out the grounds at Shattuck-St.Mary's private high school in Faribault, Minn. We were impressed it had a rink where pro alumni came and practiced.

At our first practice, we were in the locker room putting on our gear. I had to ask my buddies what I was supposed to put on first and how exactly to do that. That was my first lesson. Man, there's a lot of stuff! Swimmers just have a swimsuit, goggles and a towel! Simple.

We got to the rink in gear and Luke, one of the coaches who reminded me of *Kojak*'s Telly Savalas, took my video camera away from me. I had intended to capture all of these great moments of Collin for my wife, myself and Collin to enjoy! He then said to the camera, "Collin, now do what we tell you to do and not what your dad is about to do, for we are going to learn and practice edges." He then laughed. What am I missing?

Edges, really, why do you need to learn that? Turning is a waste of time. Just go forward from one end to the next, I said. It was a nice try on my part, but Luke sent me out. My first turn put me right on my side, back, butt, maybe all of the above! And Luke captured it all with my video camera for me, Katie and Collin to relive as much as we wanted.

It was indeed the longest hour or more of my life. Yet, each of the coaches took the time to teach me as much as they could throughout the whole time we were there. That is a testament to how great they were and made this experience.

I made it through my first practice. We hung our gear up in the locker room with a HUGE commercial fan or two to dry them out and headed up to eat before some downtime in the dorms.

Our room had two dorm beds with our sleeping bags and pillows. I had brought a HUGE fan and a cooler with snacks and drinks. I also packed some entertainment like a putting green with auto-return. It was great for playing in the hallways. We used our dirty clothes for the backstop! We also played soccer, bocce ball and baseball, among other things.

But that first night, sitting in the room with Collin, was truly a lifetime memory for me. We sat in the dark and saw that the kids during the school year had put up glow-in-the-dark stars on the ceiling. We discussed what constellations might be in the made-up star system and about the day and how much fun it was. We did this every night, and this one-on-one bonding time with Collin was the best part of the whole trip for me!

Day two. Again with the gear, and I almost got it on right the first time. It was another tough practice with games and competitions. The dads on the losing team had to do push-ups in hockey gear with their sons sitting on their backs. Collin enjoyed that too much I think, and I felt sorry for our teammates. With me, they had no chance to win, even with the coaches trying to give me as much of an advantage as they could.

Pictures in gear were taken to capture the father/son teams as well as one with me and my three buddies and our sons. After this, we saw the alumni pros practicing on the other rink, so we headed over there for our sons to get autographs and pictures. Then we had free time and headed out to a field with some of the others to play baseball and other games. More friendships were kindled.

That night, I discovered there really was a dads versus dads hockey game. So, we headed out to the rink. Of course, my first time out, I was going in one direction with virtually no control and ended up running into another dad who was slightly better than me, and I ended up on the ground. Good thing for that new helmet for I hit pretty hard! But I got up and continued to play. However, when my team was going down the ice in one direction, I usually was trying to catch up coming the other way. I was really never in the game. Until the end.

Suddenly, I found myself with the puck in the attacking zone, and Coach Luke was in goal. I skated as fast as I could (man, is it tough skating and trying to keep the puck on the stick without looking down!). When I got to the blue line, I let the puck go and yelled, "LUUKE, you forgot to teach me one thing." He said, "What was that?" I said, "How to STOP!" I put all I had into it and crashed the net with him in it.

We both were laughing hysterically. The boys were banging the boards, and the dads were worried I may have hurt Coach Luke. He was fine. Funny, no one was worried about me.

After two days of two-a-day practices and an additional hour of dry-land training, my muscles were sore, and I was grateful I had brought the cooler with ice packs and pain medicine.

On the morning of the dads versus sons game, I said to the four boys at breakfast, "You know what today is all about? It's not about if I am going to fall down and give you all a good laugh. It's not whether I have the puck and you take it away from me. It's not about if you skate by me and taunt me. No, what today is all about is which of you I get to check or lay out first and how long it takes me to get all four of you!"

Mason said, "Now that's funny!" for he knew my chance of getting even one of them was slim.

However, I'm glad to report that Mason was the very first one I got in the first period. It pays to taunt them up front. After that, he stayed next to me just out of arm's reach. I had learned the art of pushing off with my skate to get started better then he thought. One down, three more to go.

It took me the whole game, but I did finally get all four of them and, man, was I tired. It took everything in me and no, I didn't get the puck to shoot or score, but that wasn't in my game plan, either.

When the game was over, I threw up my hands in triumph. I had made it! Two practices on the ice a day, one hour of dry land training every day and that dad versus dad game every single night. Not a bone was broken or sprained!

Then I see my son skating toward me to partake in my joy. But wait. Why are Mason, Tyler, and Matt coming with him? No, no, why are all of the boys in the box coming toward me? It was payback. They all hog piled on me. With every boy in hockey gear on me, I couldn't move. I guess this is what I get for giving them a hard time all week.

When I could finally get up and recover, Coach Troy and his entire team of coaches skated out to me crying for they were laughing so hard at this sportsmanship displayed by the boys. "Tom, we are impressed with you," Troy said. "Not many dads who did not know how to skate at all would have sent their son here. Or, they would have sent him but not come with him. Or, he may have come and not put on the gear each and every time and felt foolish. But you did and had a great time doing it as well as showing the boys that you can enjoy it even though you might not be the best at it. Are you coming next year?"

I said, "Troy, my check is already cut and ready for next year. Collin and I will be back for sure!"

Chapter 18

The Father-Daughter Dance

Each year at Benilde St. Margaret High School, the school hosts a father-daughter dance. It was a particularly special dance when Alexa and Tori were seniors.

As part of the dance, the dads of the seniors prepare a special choreographed number that is presented during the dance. Those dads go to the school for a practice session and are then told what the theme for that year's dance is. We are given instructions that this is our time to shine and embarrass our daughters as much as we can with our dance costumes.

Say no more. That's exactly what I did.

However, you need to know that I have no rhythm, and I can't dance. All that practice pretty much went in one leg and out the other. I did try my best at each one though. And there was one special year where both Alexa and Tori were with me.

For Alexa's senior year, the theme was Hawaiian Barbie. I went to Ragstock and bought a Hawaiian shirt, grass hat, pink Barbie doll sunglasses and a variety of other obnoxious accessories. I looked marvelous, if I say so myself, and she loved it. The dance went off as I expected, but we had a great time.

By Tori's last two years, I had perfected the art of the outfit while having a blast. We both pondered over what we could do for the father-daughter picture taken at each dance to make all the other daughters and dads envious. For the year with the movie awards theme, we grabbed an "Oscar" which I "presented" to Tori. Her look of surprise and happiness was awesome, and we overheard many girls say, "That's a great picture; I want to do something like that!"

For her senior year, the theme was a western one. So I went and found all of the stuff we still had from our family dude ranch vacation hoping it still fit. It did: cowboy hat, rancher gloves, cowboy boots and jeans. I added some cool sunglasses and a bandana to complete the ensemble.

When I came out for her to see, Tori loved it, and you could tell many other girls pointed me out to those around them. Since I was up on the balcony and the girls were down below, I could only imagine what they were saying. Tori let me know that they were wondering whose dad I was and thought I looked really cool.

Once again, our picture was the envy of many. I grabbed the rustic wooden sign giving directions to faraway cities, brought it over to the picture area, leaned up against it and pointed to her like she was the bomb, which she was! I actually heard several girls standing in line saying, "WOW, that's a great picture!"

So dads, you don't need to know how to dance in order to have a great time with your daughters at a dance event. Use your imagination to its fullest and you're sure to capture moments that both of you will remember for a lifetime!

Pray for Me, And I'll Pray for You

Being a Catholic school, Benilde-St. Margaret's had prayers at its events. Two that were particularly meaningful to me were these two, which I wanted to include here.

These were said before dinner at the father-daughter dance. As I listened to them being prayed, I realized how I can and do have an impact on my daughters' lives as they impact mine. These words were like a reset for me to re-evaluate things during my crazy busy life.

It's amazing how dynamic prayer can be. Even though these same words were read at each dance, they meant something different to me each time.

For Fathers to Their Daughters
Loving God, You created all the people of the world,
And know each of us by name. We thank you for our daughters.
Bless them with your love And friendship that they may grow in
Wisdom, knowledge and grace. May they love their families always
And be ever faithful to their friends. Grant this through
Christ our Lord.
Amen.

For Daughters to Their Fathers
God our Father, in your wisdom and love
You made all things. Bless our fathers.
Let the example of their Faith and love shine forth.
Grant that we, their daughters,
May honor them always
With love and respect. Grant this through
Christ our Lord.
Amen.

Chapter 19
Up Nort' in the RV, Eh!

During my many years of watching my son and daughters at sporting events, I've come to some conclusions. You might call them opinions. I have a few of those. Two key ones are:

1. Sports potlucks can be successful without overkill. Just have everyone bring something along with paper products. It's simple and easy. By no means bring an egg bake. Kids HATE them!

2. Be the dad that cheers in the stands! Find a nickname for your player that resonates in the arena or on the field. "KUUUB" (pronounced Cube) is a great one for Collin Kubinksi. I know he can hear it because Collin gave me a gag order years ago, and then later told me it was okay to start using it again.

I also believe in having fun. I know. Shocking.

For one of Collin's hockey tournaments, three dads and I rented a recreational vehicle for the trip. The tournament was in Roseau, Minnesota, a good four-hour drive at least. We didn't plan on sleeping in it because the winters are extremely cold up there, and there was not enough room to fit us all. We just used it as transportation.

The crew we rented the RV from, well, it was a little like visiting the crew from the movie *Deliverance*. The RV left a little to be desired as well. The TV and video player didn't really work, the collapsible table didn't stay up very well, and we had to pour antifreeze in the toilet for "number one" and couldn't use it at all for "number two." We tried to upgrade, but it was the only RV left. Hey, we figured, it's all part of the adventure! And we only needed it to get up and back. So we took it.

We went to my house and loaded it up with all the goodies we bought: a huge tub of cheese balls, boxes of hot chocolate, candy (no nuts), meats, breads, ramen noodles, macaroni and cheese, water, sports drinks, plus a lot of wipes to clean up, and garbage bags. When all was said and done, it looked like we were going camping for a month!

Our trip up north was during an actual snowstorm where you could not see more than about three car lengths in front of you. I did most of the driving while the other dads co-piloted. Meanwhile, the boys set up the bed in the back with their knee hockey game (yes, it's really a thing) and played nearly nonstop with only short breaks for sustenance.

We finally made it to Roseau and found our hotel. We unpacked the necessities and left the rest in the RV.

The next morning, we had an early game, so our six boys ate breakfast and got their gear on. Then they asked if their teammates could ride in the RV with us to the rink. I said, "The more, the merrier." We must have had about fifteen or more of them in there! As I waited for one of the other dads to join me, I soon realized they had left me and the RV behind. Each of the other dads thought one of the other dads was riding with me.

Since I had never been to the tournament arena before, I had only general knowledge of where to go but headed out. The point was to have fun and get the boys psyched up for the game. I turned on the tunes and played "We are the Champions," "Another One Bites the Dust," "Stairway to Heaven" and whatever else they wanted to hear. They were PUMPED up at 6 a.m.

I got lost. All you could see was this HUGE RV driving around trying to find the rink. I figured that since I had over half the team, they would have to track me down sooner or later. I did eventually get unlost.

The kids loved the RV and wanted to ride in it all the time, which they did while we were up there.

When it was time to head back to the cities, it was a repeat of the boys setting up the bed in back of the RV with knee hockey tournaments galore. As we got close to home, the boys saddened for they didn't want it to be over, they had that much fun!

It was such a hit that Collin wanted to do it again for another tournament. Yet, we decided it was best to leave this memory as it was and not try to repeat it with a different team but instead make memories in other ways.

Chapter 20
Pillow Fight of the Century

As you've probably discerned, I am a LOUD, OBNOXIOUS and FUN dad. One never knows what I will do next (not even me)!

On this particular trip, my son and I headed up to Fargo with Will, one of Collin's teammates. The whole trip up was as tame as could be, but once we got to the hotel, events started unfolding quite nicely. Will was sitting on the bed getting things situated when I asked him, "What are you doing?"

He and Collin looked at me and didn't know what I was talking about. I told Will that his parents had asked me to bring him up with us but did not pay for any part of the hotel stay, so he would have to sleep in the bathtub. I got up, pulled out extra blankets and pillows from the closet, and proceeded to lay them down in the tub.

Both my son and Will's eyes got bigger as I called him and said, "Okay, it's time to go to bed since you cannot watch the TV either." I have to admit, he took it all in stride. He went in, closed the door and did not come out for a long time. So long, in fact, that Collin and I had to ask each other if he thought I was serious. Eventually, I went in and told him I was just kidding and that he could sleep in the other bed but had better keep all this stuff in the bathroom in case I changed my mind. He left it there.

All was going well until the next morning. I woke up around 5 or

5:30 a.m. and did not want to wake the boys, so I just laid there with my head facing away from them. When they woke up, Will quietly suggested that he and Collin start a pillow fight with me without warning.

When I travel, I bring my two heavy pillows. I had already reached for them and was lying in wait. When they got about one foot away from the bed, I reared up and yelled while swinging the pillows.

Will's face and reaction were priceless: "Noooo! Runnn!" And the game was afoot. Pillows were flying; bodies were being thrown onto beds; arms, legs, and heads were bouncing all over the place. Laughter came from the depths of our souls.

I WON that battle and taught them a lesson. You never know if I'm paying attention and, if so, what will come next! Good times had by all.

Chapter 21
Difficult Situations and Other Unfriendlies

In life, we have experienced bad coaches, friends, teachers, bosses, coworkers and clients. It is a fact of life. It will be no different for our kids. I want my kids to know this in advance as well as how to handle it. One piece of advice I've given them is that, if they decide to try out for a sport, activity or job, they should stick with it no matter what because they took the place of someone else who also wanted it. As long as you are learning to be better and improving, you need to take the good with the bad.

The only exception to this is if you are being attacked or bullied. I have no patience for such a thing, and I will never let someone bully my kids or make them feel bad about themselves or who they are. I will talk to my kids first to make sure they are okay with it, then I will come in with a vengeance.

Why do I feel so strongly? I grew up with two different colored eyes. I figure I got my blue eye from my father's genes and my brown eye from my mother's. It was a constant anxiety for me as I got into fights at the bus stop, got teased mercilessly and was made to feel odd. But my mom handled the situation beautifully. She told me I was special and that all of the other kids were just jealous they didn't have different colored eyes. It worked. I decided it was a gift and have never looked back.

There were two situations in my kids' lives where I felt intervention needed to happen. The first was with my oldest daughter at a dance studio. It seemed that one of the dance instructors seemed to teach with an almost militant "break them down and build them up" type of culture.

Alexa had been dancing for about ten years and really loved it. In fact, it was a great thing for both our daughters as it allowed them to gain self-confidence and come out of their shells. They would put on dance shows for family members, friends and people they had just met.

One year, however, something odd happened. For a couple dances, she was in back, the basic indication that she wasn't doing very well. But then for other dances, she was in the front line. Katie and I couldn't figure it out. We also both noticed the militant-like instruction and how it seemed to be wearing on Alexa.

We sat Alexa down and asked her how she was doing and told her what we had noticed. During the talk, we asked her if she would be okay with us setting up a meeting with the studio owner to discuss it and promised her that it would in no way negatively affect her. In fact, we felt it would make things better. After considering it for a time, she agreed.

Katie and I set up the meeting knowing that having a dad involved was uncommon in these types of talks. I had hoped that my coming would send a message that we were serious and needed to address some issues.

On the day of our meeting, I was in my car heading toward the dance studio when my wife called and told me that she had gotten there early and that I didn't need to come. She had it covered. I said, "Great for you, but I am having my talk." I needed to hear for myself what was going on and read the owner's body language while I shared my concerns and conviction that something needed to be done.

When I got there, I asked:

How, after all these years with all the time, energy, effort and money invested in this, could she be that bad? And if she was that bad, perhaps the studio and its staff had failed her.

Had the owner ever evaluated our daughter for herself to see if what was being said was true?

Could there be a personality conflict between one of the instructors and our daughter?

I shared that I was of a mind to pull Alexa out of this altogether for it was making her feel bad about herself, and that I would not stand for.

The owner replied back thoughtfully, which helped me keep an open mind. She said something like, "Well, Tom and Katie, you could take her out, but I want to ask you what message is that sending her? That whenever something is not going her way, it's okay to quit?"

Well, she hit that one on the head. It was what I had told all three of our kids about sticking it out. Yet, I also added that feeling bad about yourself is not okay and is an acceptable reason for quitting.

She then told me about a girl she had instructed for many, many years. The girl was not great but kept coming back year after year. She was in the back row for every dance. So, the owner sat down with the girl and asked the girl if she was okay with that and why she continued. The girl replied that she didn't care where she was for any performance; she just LOVED to dance. Wow. That hit home for me and it was something we had never asked Alexa.

We headed home and sat down with our daughter. We informed her that the owner was going to evaluate things and get back to us. And, we asked her the same questions the owner had asked that other girl. Alexa, why are you dancing? Does it really matter where you are in the dance? Do you strive to be front and center; is that important to you?

She replied quickly saying she didn't care where she was in the dance; she just loved doing it and had great friends. Sometimes it would be nice to be in a better position, she added, but she knew which dances she was good at and which dances others were better at. She was okay with that. I was so proud when I heard her answers!

Having Alexa realize what was important to her and sticking it out as the champion she is was one of my proud father moments. She persevered, didn't whine, didn't tattle and had a great year. She handled it in her own way. And her answer was spot on. Keep it up Alexa and you'll accomplish so much in your lifetime. You are amazing!

Tori, our other daughter found herself in a similar situation during college. All along we have tried to help our kids self-advocate and, at this age, it was very important that she try first on her own before we provided assistance, if she needed and wanted it, provided she was not being bullied or made to feel bad about herself.

Talk about IMPRESSIVE! She took the bull by the horns and met with her coaches and the athletic director to discuss her situation. She was on point, offered anecdotal information on what she had done to address a concern, and then stated how she felt the results were not handled appropriately. I have never been so PROUD of her as when she informed us of the actions she had taken and what she had said.

The results were not as good as she or we had hoped for, but she truly is a WOMAN in charge of her own destiny, not willing to sit by and just let it happen without addressing it and fighting for what she believes to be right! Way to go, TORI!

Protect them when you need to!
Fight the battles you need to fight on their behalf.
Let them fight the ones that they need to.
Let them grow and blossom.
Don't be a helicopter parent!

Chapter 22
Things Don't Always Go As Planned

During Tori's second year in college, she suffered a terrible sports injury, a compound break in her left leg during a competition dance practice.

She handled it like a champ though for the rest of the season and school year. She went to every single practice and watched as an alternate in hopes the injury would heal in time for Nationals at year's end.

I knew that going to class and getting around was going to be extremely difficult for her. So I picked up the phone to see what the university could do to lighten the burden for her. I spoke to the dean of admissions, security, housing and many others as the university guided me along the way. The plan then was to have security talk to Tori about transportation to and from classes and back to her room. The school also provided additional benches in her room so she could prop up her leg as needed.

The resident assistant was told about the situation and agreed to check in on Tori on a regular basis to make sure she didn't need anything, and her professors made arrangements to help her get makeup tests and homework. All in all, the university was very accommodating.

Yet, we still needed to get her out of the hospital and on her path to recovery. So, I drove up to the St. Cloud hospital and stayed with her for about a week's time. After chatting with the doctors and nurses about her recovery plan, I created an agenda.

We set goals for her to get out of bed and apply pressure in stages so that she could begin trying to walk. Tori would get up about every hour on the hour and just sit on the edge of the bed and then stand up and apply pressure to the leg. Each time, she stood and applied pressure a little bit longer.

Then we set goals for Tori to actually walk a few steps at a time. Our first goal was to get from her bed to the doorway. Then it was from the doorway to the nurses' station. Then from the doorway past the nurses' station to the hallway. The ultimate goal was to walk all the way from her room down the hall to the coffee station and then back again. It took about a week to get that far along with all of the physical therapy the hospital was doing.

I was very concerned for her and how she was doing. I used tough love several times to push her, and I was starting to feel I was being too tough on her. However, one of the nurses pulled me aside in the hall as I was going for coffee and told me that I was a great dad and doing all the right things with Tori. If I wasn't tough on her, it would only hurt her in the long run and she wouldn't recover as well as she could. Man, that brought relief to my whole being when she said that!

So, we hunkered down and kept pressing on. I missed the final goal of her walking all on her own from her room, past the nurses' station, past all those hallway markers, to the coffee area and then all the way back to her room. The nurse pulled me aside and said Tori wanted to surprise me with it, and she did! I thought, "Way to go honey! You are one tough cookie, and I am so PROUD of you for staying positive and getting through this."

After reaching that milestone, we then headed back to the university. She had crutches now and my next goal for her was to use those less and less.

So, I asked her to take me to one of her classes, which was art. She was sketching a collage and then painting it, and I couldn't wait to see what she had done so far.

As we got out of the car, I said, "Why don't you walk as far as you can while I hold onto your crutches?" She thought about it awhile and said, "Okay. Let's try it." As we walked, I was close by but far enough away that she could not reach for the crutches. About halfway there, she asked for them back, and I said, "You know, you're doing really well. Let's try for a bit further." We set a goal and kept moving that goal further and further until she realized that she was at the classroom.

"Wow," she said, "I didn't think I could do it." I told her that if she just broke it down to little goals along the way in all she did, she could accomplish anything. It's when you look at the whole picture that it seems overwhelming.

Things progressed slowly for her, but she never complained and handled the challenge every single day. She even carried her crutches most of the day in order to push her injury healing quicker so she could get back to a normal life.

Try as she might, though, the injury just would not heal completely. She couldn't stand on it for a long period of time, walk great distances, jump, leap or do other movements one does in pretty much any sport.

How difficult that is for any athlete! To be part of something and yet not really able to participate. That takes a truly tough individual to be able to do that.

As the summer went on, Tori realized that a major part of the reason why she had chosen that university was dance competition. It was her social group, sorority, sisterhood where she had her teammates and friends. They spent a ton of time practicing but also socializing. Even going to the football games where she and her team performed at halftime was lost to her.

She came to both Katie and I and said that she was considering switching schools for her junior and senior years because her current school just made her sad. She had already taken it upon herself to research Iowa State, which had been her second choice when she graduated high school. She found out which classes she would not receive credit for, which ones she would need to take in order to continue her major and how to rush for the sororities she wanted to join.

As the negotiator that she is, Tori had even gone back to the pros and cons list we had first created when helping decide which university to go to in the first place. She then showed me that most of the pros for College of St. Benedict were now gone and that Iowa State now had them. (This list is more fully discussed in chapter 29, College Prep.)

It really seemed she had thought this all out! She had done her homework and had sound reasons for transferring. How could we say no to her after all of that? Even though I would have been scared to move and start all over a new with just two years left, she had no problems with it.

We are very PROUD of her! The STRONG and INDEPENDENT WOMAN she has become—to self-advocate like that! Not many college sophomores are able to so clearly delineate their reasons or to stand up for themselves so well which tells you she will be a HUGE success in life.

She not only is thriving there, but will graduate on time and has a wonderful significant other in her life.

Well done, Tori! You are truly amazing to me, and I am PROUD to be able to call you my daughter and I your father!

So dads, sometimes you need to know when to apply TOUGH LOVE no matter how much it may hurt us to do it—when to push them while standing beside them all the way, when to pick them up, support them and be their biggest fan and cheerleader.

Yet, you also need to know that, when they are all grown up and capable of making their own difficult decisions, you've done your job by giving them the tools they need and now you need to let go, no matter how hard that is. At times, I find myself asking, "Where did all the time go?" One minute they're little and then WHAM! They're young adults.

Chapter 23
Visitors from Japan

When our girls were in high school, the opportunity arose to have a foreign exchange student from a Japanese private high school for a week. Katie and I wanted all of our kids to be able to experience either traveling out of the country, having visitors from out of the country or both in their lifetimes. Opening your home to someone from a different country can really give you something to cherish forever. So, we all talked about it and what our individual responsibilities would be. All three kids were on board with the idea and excited!

We let the exchange program know we would love to take advantage of the experience, and they called back with an opportunity to have not one but two girls. We thought that this would be great for the exchange students. If one or both didn't speak English very well, they could try and work through the language differences, and they would have someone else here to converse with. Plus, we all could have double the experience!

The school put together a class to help the host families and students learn something about the language and culture before the exchange students arrived. I attended each one. In addition, I went to the bookstore and bought a Fodor translation book so we could have Post-It notes on various things throughout the house in both English and Japanese. To my surprise, though, when the girls came to our home, they did not understand the words because they were written in English characters! It took a bit to figure out, but we all laughed about the attempt on my part.

Once they arrived, the students had their class schedules, pre-planned events, and events for their host families to attend. Then, during free days, we as a family could supplement those experiences with truly Minnesotan adventures. We got to meet "our girls": Saeko and Yumi. Saeko liked pizza, shopping and playing basketball. Yumi liked fantasy and mystery novels and small animals like cats.

We toured college campuses, took a Mississippi River boat ride, did some shopping at the Mall of America, and visited the Minneapolis Institute of Arts and Minneapolis Sculpture Garden. A highlight was the time at the Renaissance Festival! It was filled with eye-opening moments: people-watching, shopping, rides like a gigantic rocking horse, and unique foods they just had to try. We actually met Ruth Thompson, the medieval dragon artist. And they got to be honorary queens for the day when they donned the crowns at a shop. They loved it!

While at our home, we initiated them into the world of s'mores as we sat in our backyard by the fire pit. It actually became a nightly routine no matter what time we got back home or what the weather conditions were. They couldn't get enough of them and averaged three per night!

We also enjoyed sparklers, billiards, and soccer games as spectators.

As for culinary delights, we had St. John's Bread turned into the most awesome French bread ever! We also enjoyed pancakes shaped like Mickey Mouse, butterflies, snowmen and anything else we wanted. Saeko and Yumi even cooked some up. And, when in Minnesota, make sure you stop at Snuffy's Malt Shop. They also enjoyed Kobe, our neighborhood Japanese restaurant.

Our family had a chance to get to know some of the other students a little, too, when we joined the ice skating party at the Parade Ice

Gardens. I was surprised some of them were so good, but they had had prior experience.

The Japanese characters under our stairs were left by Saeko and Yumi and is a beautiful reminder of some great girls and the memories we share. And it's neat to know how we impacted them.

On the last evening of the stay, the coordinators of the trip hosted a sayonara party with Japanese entertainment for all of us to experience. It was heartwarming and emotional for all, for they had adopted us as we had adopted them, and we hated to see the time coming to an end.

Of course, I couldn't let them go back home empty handed! So, I took all of the pictures that we had taken throughout their visit, made triplicates, and bought small photo albums for them and us. I put all of the pictures in the albums along with notes that also shared the dates and events depicted. I also purchased a small amount of s'mores items for the flight home.

They cried when they opened the gifts and gave me a HUGE hug! I cried as well and even more when I dropped them off, but don't let anyone else know that. It would ruin my big, tough image.

They each gave our family a memory book as well.

This truly was an experience of a lifetime not only for Alexa, Tori, Collin, Katie and myself, but also for Saeko and Yumi. It was everything and so much more than we had hoped it would be, and I can only hope you and your families get the same wonderful chance.

Chapter 24
Simple as a Cup of Coffee

As our kids get older, it may be more difficult for us dads to connect with our daughters than with our sons, but we can establish a fun and safe environment for them to open up and talk about what's going on in their world.

I have found simply going out for a cup of coffee (or mocha or chai latte or white peach berry smoothie...) has created many memories for just between us. We've been to coffeehouses near campus, on campus, near home and some halfway between our work places so we could have some special time together.

I found this setting allowed me and my daughters an opportunity to open up and relate to one another in a completely different way than I do with my son, which tends to be more interactive and without an emphasis on conversation. You're allowing everything to flow and come naturally.

Both Alexa and Tori have told me that these conversations help them solve problems, feel better about situations, or get a different perspective on things. They are able to get stuff off their chests if all they want to do is talk it through without having me give my solution. We also enjoy some great laughs.

Tori's strong, independent nature along with her determination to get what she wants, how she wants it and when she wants will take her far.

These traits have been evident for a long time, and her mom and I are proud of her and what she's accomplishing.

Yet, it was during these coffee breaks that I truly discovered Alexa. She is wise beyond her years and spending time with her one-on-one gave me a chance to see how she processes everything methodically before acting. It also gave me opportunity to "see" through our conversation how her loving, caring and nurturing personality defines who she is for she's always there when someone needs her. I am PROUD to call you my daughter, Alexa LU!

It's important, dads, for us to take the time to relate to each of our children in a manner that works best for them, that is comfortable and safe. And it is also important that we remember that not all problems need us to find a solution like the hunters that we are. Sometimes we just need to be that ear to bend or shoulder to cry on without saying anything.

Chapter 25
Spaghetti Squash Football

Yes, you read that right; I did say Spaghetti Squash Football.

This started out as the old time football-in-the-water game with an actual football but morphed into a Vaseline-covered watermelon which is very slippery and fun. The problem with that, though, was that the watermelon usually broke quickly from all of the roughness incurred during tug of wars.

While I was at the grocery store one day, I came across this stuff called spaghetti squash and, wouldn't you know, it looked very much like an actual football. I picked one up, and it felt like I could throw a spiral pass with it. Knocking it with my knuckles, it appeared that it would hold up to the wear, tear and abuse that we would put it through during a water football game.

Of course I purchased one, brought it to game central after filing down the stem to make it smooth, and we tested it out.

WOW! It was totally awesome and held up wonderfully. We could pass it quite well. It didn't break apart, and ever since, we use them for our annual event up north.

How does one play spaghetti squash football? I'm glad you asked.

Here are the rules.

- Buy said spaghetti squash.

- Buy petroleum jelly if you wish to apply for extra slipperiness.

- Divide players into two teams.

- Be in a lake.

- Determine boundaries for end zones and out of bounds. For us, out-of-bounds is only in the shallow end less than knee high so you don't get hurt when tackled.

- Coin toss for who starts on offense and other team passes said spaghetti squash for return.

- Once the person with the ball is tackled under water, a new down starts.

- There are four downs per turn, and you can opt to pass for a punt.

- A touchdown within four downs is a point.

- If there is no touchdown within four downs and you didn't pass for a punt, then the other team takes over from that spot.

- After each touchdown, teams go to their sides and pass for the next team to return the "ball."

- Passing is allowed when it is your four downs.

- Lateralling backward is also allowed for both returns and four downs, but be careful, for the other team could steal the spaghetti squash football and run in for a TD (touchdown).

- During the running of downs, if an opponent steals the squash out of the carrier's hands, it's an interception and it can be run back for a touchdown.

There you are, and give it a try. I hope you'll enjoy it as much as we do. It is sure to change up the old football game and move you to the waterways.

Papa Kubs scores!

Chapter 26
Apple Pie: The True Story Finally Told

Both our girls have been doing the studio dance thing since they were about four years old. Drop off and pick up duties were shared equally by me and my wife; however, during their later years, it seems I was the one regularly picking them up afterward. That could be because we always stopped at Wendy's for a frosty and fries. You can't have fries without a frosty, donchaknow!

I started asking for an apple pie at the drive up just to mess with Wendy's, because that's what I do. Each time, they'd say they didn't have apple pies. Well, then I'd ask for blueberry, raspberry, and others. Again, they don't offer them. I'd ask when they would be offering them so we would know when to ask. Silence.

Well, the girls and a friend or two of theirs were joining us quite often, and they started to ask for the apple pie. They even made up a song about apple pie and sang it to the Wendy's drive up.

That told me that I needed to take the next step, so I went and bought an apple pie for each one at another place. I brought it to Wendy's and told them who I was and what I wanted to do. They were all in! They wrapped them in Wendy's wrappers and waited for me to return.

We all drive up, and the girls started in with the song, I believe, and the manager said, "Well, we just so happen to have apple pies today."

The girls were silent. We all know how special that moment is, but it only lasted a moment, and it was gone just like that.

They, of course, had the apple pies, frosty and fries. The world was in order and life was good.

Well now, the girls were so taken by that, that we just had to go to the grocery store and buy a cake mix to make for the Wendy's crew to say thanks. So, I drove there and watched and laughed inside as they made this a HUGE event.

The next day, we drove there and all of us went in to deliver it and say thanks. The manager looked at me, and I shook my head to indicate she should just go along with it and not tell them what I did. It would be our little secret for quite some time.

Yet, it didn't stop there. The next time we headed there, they asked again and were told that was a one-time special deal only for them!

The girls shared this story for many, many years until, when they were in college, I finally let them know what I had done. You could have heard a pin drop as looks of shock and disappointment registered on their faces. I had just burst their bubble.

They didn't focus on the fact that I, their dad, loved and cared so much for them that I came up with this grand idea and did it for them. They were disappointed because they no longer felt special and singled out by the Wendy's team. I sat there wondering how to respond to them before sharing how my love for them had motivated me to go to all this effort.

I don't think they ever will forgive me for letting the cat out of the bag. My advice to you, if you do anything like this, is think twice about coming clean and being the hero. Instead, just be an unsung hero.

Chapter 27
Sign, Sign, Everywhere a Sign

If you are like me, you want to give your kids advantages when you can, especially when you feel things are skewed against them.

Such is the case for the Department of Motor Vehicle's driver's license testing station by our home. You see, they have a four-lane "highway," all one-way, that is not clearly marked. Yes, they have the white painted lines telling you that it is a one-way, but ALL streets should have signs clearly detailing this fact as well. This one does not. It got me during my test, and I was not about to let it get my kids as well.

So, my oldest daughter and I headed to the DMV and drove right into the facility and proceeded to go through EVERY road, stop sign, stop light, one way, parking spot, etc. I pointed out where the one-way was, why it was done in this manner, and what she was to do.

As we were going through these drills multiple times, I noticed the stop light had stopped working. I figured they must have had a power issue with it, so we just kept on going through the course.

Then, we rounded the corner so we could see the exit to the facility. I noticed no stop lights were working, no cars were anywhere to be seen and, to my shock, a guy was getting out of a van and pulling the gate shut.

I immediately honked our horn and had my daughter drive up to the exit. When we got there, the guy said, "NO practice driving! NO training! NO soliciting! No advertising on premises! Didn't you see the sign?" No, I hadn't seen the sign, I said. Where was it? He pointed to it. It was right as you drove in, BIG and PLAIN as day.

I said we were sorry and that it wouldn't happen again. We then left.

My daughter was mortified. "Dad, what will I do if they remember me when I come in for my test?" she said. I said the odds of that happening were slim to none and offered her use of another car for the test.

She didn't take another car and passed with flying colors.

I bet you are wondering what went through my mind as I watched him shut and lock the gate! Well, I had a solution for that, but that is another story.

As a side note, NO, I didn't take our other two kids there to practice. I wasn't allowed. So dads, do all you can to help your kids succeed, but sometimes things don't go smoothly; do what makes the best sense for your kids.

Chapter 28
You Know You've Made a Difference When...

On my fifty-first birthday, about ten of my son's friends, both boys and girls, started sending me texts wishing me a happy birthday along with some ribbing. The next night, about six of them came over to surprise me with my favorite red velvet cupcakes, complete with candles and chocolate ice cream and to sing "Happy Birthday" to me. It was a very special moment, and it told me that I had become a much better person, man and father than I ever thought I would.

Sometime later on in the year, Collin and I were sitting around talking, as we do, about life, school, sports, friends. I told him that, at his last varsity hockey game, Katie and I were walking around the stands when I photo bombed a group of girls trying to get the perfect angle and picture. As Katie and I walked away, we heard one of them saying this was the best thing that had happened to her that day, and they all laughed loudly. I had no idea who they were but knew they were from his high school.

After he was done laughing, Collin then said, out of the blue, "All my friends LOVE you!" I told him I didn't know who the girls were. He said, "Yeah, it pretty much doesn't matter. They all know about you!"

When this happens, you know that you have accomplished something very special.

Part 2

The College Years

Chapter 29
College Prep

Too fast, time has gone by, and now it's time to send your kids off to college.

529 College Funds

Don't make the same mistake we and many others have over the years by not setting up some type of college fund program early. You think you have time and will be able to catch up, but that is not always the case. I would recommend putting away something every single month for each child as soon as they are born! I cannot emphasize this enough. It can make all the difference in lightening the load, burden and overwhelming debt amount for not only them, but yourself!

We did the 529 Plan, named after the section in the Internal Revenue Service code that set it up 20 years ago. Does it need to be a 529? Only you can decide if that venue or something else works best for you. Yet, start as soon as you can, don't tap into it no matter what, and you'll be very happy you did later.

Family Quiz

Before choosing a school, you and your student should take the following quiz. Don't be surprised if your answers don't match. This is NOT a test, and it's not graded either!

- What should we look for in a college or university?

- What do we ask for information on?

- Where and how do we begin our search?

- Once decided, HOW do we make it SPECIAL for our son/daughter?

- Which school do we choose?

These are all great questions for when the time is right, and I have provided some awesome insights for how to approach each one.

Time to Start Thinking About College

Like most of us who didn't do our homework, we are not prepared, and the final is today. I remember the first time we had to consider colleges for our oldest and know exactly what you are thinking and feeling.

It is overwhelming and something none of us really thought about and figured we'd deal with it when the time came. When our second went, we had a better idea of what to do, but we still could have done some additional things. Our third is just around the corner and I think we got it pretty much under control.

That's the way it is; the more you do it, the better you get at it. Yet, something this important should be much easier the first time around.

Not to worry. Having been through this process now a few times and having worked the Minnesota State Fair college booth for St John's University and College of St. Benedict's for over six years, I have learned quite a few things that I will pass onto you for consideration.

Before we go through all of those items, I would like to suggest the following advice that I have given each of my kids. "I don't care where you go as long as you:

- Get a great education–that's number one.

- Establish good friendships.

- Build awesome life experiences.

- Have fun. However, if this takes priority, college is over for you."

So how do you go about choosing a school? Here are the questions that I asked our kids, the kids who stopped by at the education booth at the state fair and, of course, the parents. Again, ask the kids on their own, and you parents think about them as well. We cannot, and should not, pick the college for our kids. It must be their choice for them to own it and apply themselves properly. This way, they cannot blame you in any way for anything that may occur or how well they do. Their happiness and success rests solely on them and what they do or don't do.

What three things are most important to you when looking for a college or university?

- A small, medium or large campus?

- Small or large enrollment?

- An urban or rural campus?

- What course of study do you plan to pursue? (Keep in mind many underclassmen do change their majors at least once.)

- What benchmarks do you have for the school's athletics?

- Do you want to play on a college team, club sport or other? What are your chances of making the team? Remember, you are here to get an education first.

- What expectations or wants do you have for the living quarters?

- What extra-curricular activities are you interested in?

- Do you need a meal plan?

- Does the school have an alumni network and networking opportunities?

Ask the University

Here are questions you and your student can ask when on visits.

Safety

- What security systems are in place around campus, dorms, buildings?

- Do all buildings require an ID badge, security code? Do they have cameras and locking doors?

- Do you have emergency posts throughout the grounds?

- How many attacks/assaults to the female population have there been over the past three years?

- How many robberies have there been annually during the past three years?

- How many security officers are on campus, and how often do they patrol areas?

- What is the lighting like at night around campus?

What percent of students graduate in their:

- Fourth year

- Fifth year

- Sixth year

Cost for tuition, books, meals, housing, and miscellaneous spending

4 years will cost approximately: _____

5 years will cost approximately: _____

6 years will cost approximately: _____

How much debt does a student typically graduate away with?

What scholarships do you have based on?

- Grades

- SAT or ACT scores

- Work programs

- Grants

- Fellowships

- Sports

- Others offered

Living

- What types of housing do you have: dorms, houses, frats, earth homes, etc.?

- Which living spaces have air conditioning in rooms versus not?

- Is it co-ed?

- In what year do you qualify for each?

- What percent of the student body gets them each year?

- Can you live off campus?

- If you can live off campus, what percentage can and do?

- What size are the dorm rooms?

- Do dorm rooms have an air conditioner?

- Do dorm rooms have views?

- What amenities do dorm rooms come with?

- Dorm room needs: what can we put in them?

- Where is the safest place to live both on and off campus?

Income

- On average, how much does a student spend in a month on extras?

- What part time jobs are available on campus?

- How much do they pay?

- What percentages of students get them?

- How do you decide who gets them?

- What are the hours?

Student Body

- What is the size of total student body?

- Number of Freshmen? Sophomores? Juniors? Seniors?

- Ratio of women to men in each class

- Average number of students per class room

What medical services do you have on campus?

- Nurse? Doctor? Pharmacy? Clinic?

Is there a community on campus? If so, what is the community known for?

Students

Here are some questions your prospective student should be asking current students when they visit.

What are the top three things you would change about this school?

What is it like on the weekends here—do most students go home, stay? What activities are there? Is it fun?

What were the big controversial issues on campus last year?

Do you know anyone who was attacked or robbed last year?

Questions Student Athletes Should Ask

When I was recruited for division one swimming way back in my day, I had no idea what questions to ask or what to look for to make an informed decision. Luckily, I did figure out early on what was important to me so I could make the best decisions for myself, and it paid off wonderfully throughout my life.

I now have three children who also are student athletes, so I put together a quick reference sheet as a starting point for them. Students should also review the prior list; some of those community and safety questions are important to ask, too, when coaches come calling. And put the key information into your cell phone so if the coach calls when you're not at home, you still have the info for easy reference.

Coaches Calling: What to Say, Ask, Do

Date _____

University/College _____

Coach Name _____

Phone Number _____

Next Steps

Set up tour date: _____

Call back date:

Other: _____

- How did you hear about me? What prompted you to reach out to me today?

- What do you look for in a student athlete? Area of interest in major? Grades? The sport itself? Ability?

- Does playing multiple sports help or hinder anything?

- How does playing juniors before my first year of college factor in?

- What is the season timeline?

  Captain's practice date start:

  Season itself starts:

  Regions:

  Sections:

  Nationals:

- Practice itself

  How many times a day?

  How long is each practice?

  Will I have time to study?

- What's the average number of years players on your team are at the university?

- What percent graduate in four years? Five years?

- Does red shirting or holding back play a part? And if so, would it be for me?

- Where do athletes live on campus? Do they stay in the same dorm or house? Or do they live where they want?

- Where would I fit within your team, and how much playing time would you expect me to see each year?

- Is there anything you feel I should be working on, focusing on this next season?

- What types of scholarships are there for:

  Athletics?

  Grades?

  Grants?

  Whom do I contact to see if I would receive any of these?

- Since this process is all new to me, is there anything I should ask about but didn't?

At the end of the call, thank the coach for reaching out to you and emphasize how honored you are to receive the call. Then ask what the next step is and when to follow up.

What are the colleges' stand-out attributes?

When we began looking at St. John's University and College of St. Benedict, we found information we catalogued as important. Perhaps these will assist you and provide ideas of what to be looking for and asking about.

How does this school provide a unique learning experience?

What is the setting like? What kind of ambience does it provide?

What types of buildings are there?

What kinds of values and traditions are highly regarded?

How many faculty are there? What percent have the highest degree available in their field?

What academic programs does it have? What majors and minors are available?

What is the student to faculty ratio?

What is the average class size?

- This was a HUGE one for me. When I was recruited by a division one school, the average class size was 30–50 students or more. In fact, one had more than 300 and was taught by TV monitor with no professor present. And, on average, it took five to six years to graduate.

How many students take advantage of study-abroad opportunities?

How many classes have an international component?

On average, how many years does it take a student to graduate?

How many students are enrolled? How many men? How many women? How many are from other countries?

Career Development

At SJU and CSB, Career Services sponsors numerous programs, workshops and other services to help students from their first year all the way through their senior year as they choose majors, explore careers, gain relevant work experience and plan for life after graduation. More than 8,100 graduates have volunteered to assist students with career exploration, internships and potential employment. The office also hosts a series of weekly panel discussions with graduates to showcase a wide array of career fields.

Costs

What we found fascinating is that the average student at a state university takes at least five years to graduate. When you are calculating costs, you then need to add in one more year of tuition, books, room, board, et cetera.

In addition, we found that private universities, once financial aid and grants are made available, are actually about one-third cheaper than the stated tuition costs. Private universities may cost about 15 percent less.

College Navigator (nces.ed.gov/collegenavigator) is a great resource! It shows the percent of students at university receiving financial aid and merit awards given out. Just type in the name of the university and find:

- percent of students getting financial aid, grants, university loans

- the academic profile of admitted students

- the number of students in each major

- graduation rates for four, five and six years

- a calculator for total costs for four, five and six years

To narrow a search, you can also enter your own variables.

There is a common data set that every school has posted. Pay attention to the financial aid section. You can look at the financial aid to the more affluent as well as need-based aid.

Collegeboard.com, Fiske Guide and Princeton Review are services that can help match you to colleges. They also can help you prep for ACT and SAT tests. Scholaredge.com can help provide strategies on getting into top level private schools. Fastweb.com also has some great resources like articles and many scholarships for which you can apply on their site.

For more college strategies, sign up for thecollegesolutions@gmail.com email newsletter.

You can track financial aid issues through finaid.org.

If your household experiences unusual circumstances such as a lost job or major medical issue, contact the school and notify them. You can also ask for additional assistance.

When paying for school, make sure you use the free money, like grants and scholarships, first. Most schools use the FAFSA (Free Application for Federal Student Aid) application at fafsa.ed.gov. (Other web sites exist to "help" you do FAFSA but then charge you. The official government site is free!) This requires the parents and students to enter their income information. What's nice is that the government just changed it so you can use the "prior-prior" year's taxes when filling it out. For example, in 2017, you can now use tax info from your 2015 return. Once you've completed the application, an email will tell you for what grants you are eligible. Make sure you also send this data to your school choices.

When filling out FAFSA, you are not required to input data on retirement information like IRA or 401k information or home equity. **This is important that you don't include it in applications!** And don't repeat information. If you do, it's counted twice.

After you exhaust the grants and scholarships, then move on toward federal school loans which offer fixed interest rates along with regular payments, deferred payments and debt forgiveness. Private loans are harder to get and you can pay interest-only while you're in school, but they're not as flexible.

Final College Choices—What To Do

When your children get down to their final two choices, have them stay at each one overnight on a weekday and night so they can see what the community life is like during a study day. Then, have them stay at each one overnight during the weekend so they can see what the community life is like then. They will be different, and it's the only way they will know if they fit, can fit, like it or don't want any part of it. You can set this up by calling the admissions office at the colleges. They have students willing to house prospective students overnight. It really helped our girls choose between two really close options.

When they were choosing between the schools, I reiterated that I wouldn't tell them which school to go to, but I would:

• Ask them what they liked about each one and how the two schools compared.

• Ask what they didn't like about each one.

• Sit down with that child and look at the big picture. I recommend drawing up a "T account" where you draw a vertical line down the center of the paper. Then write the name of each school at the top of the sheet, one on each side of the vertical line. Beneath the names then draw a horizontal line to separate the school name from the rest of the page. Underneath each school, draw another vertical line so each school now has two sections. In the left section, write "Pros." In the right section under each school, write "Cons." Then list out the positives and negatives of each school.

When you're done, have them ask themselves which school their heart is telling them is right for them. Keep all of this paperwork for future reference in case of buyer's remorse.

Finally, type up an agreement about who is paying for what and go over it with them so they know and understand expectations. In our case, my wife and I listed our expectations for our child's grade point average. If they obtained a certain average, we would assist with a certain dollar amount toward loan payments. We wanted to make sure they had some of their own money invested in their education but not so much that they were burdened or overwhelmed. We also expected them to work a certain number of hours for their own spending money.

Buyer's Remorse

We all have experienced buyer's remorse with decisions we have made. It is no different with our kids in regard to selecting the college they attend. It's a crazy time—being away on your own for the first time, learning how to live with someone you may or may not know, how to set study habits, meeting and making new friends, managing money, doing your work program and basically learning about life all on your own.

If your child ever calls and is not sure they made the right decision, here is what I have said.

- Go back to all you did to decide to go here. What did you decide in your heart and why?

- What, if anything, has changed since doing all of that?

- Are you just overwhelmed and maybe missing home where life was simpler?

As I have told each child, once you make a decision, you need to stick it out for the full season, term, etc. It can change, and as long as you give it your all, do your best and learn something or become better, you can make a different decision next time. Yet, keep in mind that all the uncertainties you had for this one will be the same next time, and then you'll have buyer's remorse about what you left and knew after a year.

Even I had buyer's remorse on my first year, but found a GREAT LIFE EXPERIENCE.

I am glad to say that both our daughters LOVED their first years so much they didn't want to come home when it was over, even after going through buyer's remorse in year one.

Chapter 30
And They're Off: Making It Special

Once your child has chosen a school, there are a couple things you can do to help give them a leg up.

What Your Student Can Do

1. Have your student get a banking account and debit card. Have them learn how to balance it and make sure the charges are all theirs.

2. Identity theft does occur; set limits on the debit card on what can be taken out without approval from the account owner.

3. Have your student take a personal finance course to help with budgeting and using forms of payment.

What You Can Do

First, buy them a college safety AND basic needs basket. Okay, it has to be a big basket. In it, include:

- flashlight and batteries

- smoke detector and batteries, carbon monoxide detector that plugs into the wall

- fire extinguisher, escape ladder, and two plans of escape from the living space

- hand sanitizers and cleaning wipes

- laundry detergent, softener, fabric sheets, bag, basket

- toiletries: soap, shampoo, conditioner, curling iron, hair dryer, toothbrush, soap holder, toothpaste

- laptop-carrying case, charger, mouse, mouse pad

- stapler, tape, ruler, pens, pencils, scissors, paper clips, paper, calculator

- fan, sound machine, electrical cords

- rugs, lights, lamp

- backpack

Once they're on campus and mostly on their own, it's time for you to add just a little extra.

Making It Special

We all remember that getting mail or packages at college was HUGE, exciting and MADE OUR DAY—especially if we had had a bad one! Let's not forget about making classmates and friends jealous that we got something special. And, when doing this for our kids, it's even better if you do it in a recurring cycle versus just once in a great while.

Here are some things I have done that were fun for both them and myself. Check them out and make them your special events.

Alexa's Freshman Year

Send a card every single week.

Later on in this book is a section that includes the notes I sent to Alexa and later to Tori to give you an idea of what you can write about. Feel free to use parts for yours if you wish.

Some of the best cards I sent that first year were a girl on a bicycle with her doll house because she was moving (and don't come back! LOL) and a card that looked like a purse. Of course, I put some cold hard cash for the starving and broke college student.

Send a CARE package once a month.

Fill it with all kinds of stuff. The Dollar Store has great knick knacks and HOLIDAY items well in advance of the holiday so your student has something to decorate her room with, etc. She started to keep a bin to hold all of her holiday items and brought it to school each year to use and add to as I sent them. Costco had awesome bulk items for her to share with her roommates and friends. The CandyLand store was great for popcorn and, of course, candies. Send whatever it is that you know they will like and enjoy.

Alexa placed all the cards on her wall so everyone could see them. I saw them, and it made me very happy. Her friends said I was the best dad, and I received many pictures of them enjoying the snacks I sent.

Well into her freshman year, I started to include some of her clothes as well saying that I had rented her room out to another girl who needed more closet space. I wanted to get a friend to come over with her suitcase and take a picture of her sitting on Alexa's bed with a contract and check but, sadly, I was not able to make it happen.

Interestingly enough, Alexa called me when her first batch of clothes arrived in the monthly care package and said, "That's not funny, Dad."

But we both laughed and it became a recurring joke for awhile. Yet, it seems I sent so many clothes over time, that I needed to bring an extra suitcase to bring them back!

Sophomore Year

As we were getting Alexa settled that second year, she turned to me and said, "Dad, I know exactly where I am going to put all those cards you send me."

I said, "That was a lot of work finding all of those great cards and figuring out what to say. I don't know if I have it in me to do it all again this year."

She looked at me; she knew me better than that. I had already planned on doing it and had the first one in the mail on its way to her to arrive the next day. It's great to know all of that really made a difference.

Junior Year

Alexa's junior year was also my daughter Tori's freshman year at college. As we were getting Tori unpacked at school, she said to me, "Dad, I know where I am going to put all of those cards you send me like you did Alexa."

Holy schnikey, what did I get myself into? Can you imagine not only trying to find the perfect card now for two daughters, but writing them each something every week of their college days?

The Monthly CARE packages are no brainers and easy, but card hunting and writing, now that is another story!

Well, I managed to do just that. Two cards every single week and two care packages every month.

The pictures of both of them with their friends enjoying the care packages said it all as did seeing the cards displayed when I visited.

Chapter 31
Studying Abroad

One would think that you'd get a break from the letters and packages and creativity when your child studies abroad, but not this dad. I asked her for her mailing address way before she left so I could surprise her when she got there. Yep, that is correct. When she got to her flat and met all of her fellow flatmates, she was informed that she had some mail and a package for her.

Pictures came to me with the caption, "I got a package." More came as her flatmates enjoyed the items that I sent that they could not get in London and were favorites here in the good old USA: Oreos, Jif peanut butter, animal cookies, Kraft Mac'n Cheese, ramen noodles, candy, etc.

If your child is studying abroad, I would recommend that you and your child make a spreadsheet for this well in advance so you can track the progress of things needing to be done in a timely manner and ensure nothing gets forgotten. It can be daunting the first time, but it can also make a real difference in their enjoyment and provide peace of mind for you knowing that you have done all you could to ensure fun and safety.

For the Task/Description column, the things I took notes on were:

University's information meeting

Weekly update meetings via phone/FaceTime with student and parents

Monthly meeting with Ambassador or previous study abroad students

Register for housing, classes, and internship, medical

Financial aid needed?

Medical appointment to make sure vaccines are up to date

Check Center for Disease Control website for travel location

Insurance coverage—homeowner's theft of cell phone, computer, renters insurance, etc.

Medical insurance coverage while there and what to do if needed, how to handle claim

Emergency evacuation for medical reasons (make sure insurance covers, process to follow)

Bank—alert them that you are going, what cards to have, minimum/maximum balances in case cards are stolen or lost, and cash

Cell phone—options, disposable phone, buy minutes, etc.

Camera—do they need or want one? The smaller the better

Host family for one week: check them out

State department: register both student and parents for updates

AAA membership for books, maps, assistance for traveling

Buy: travel guide book, prescriptions, micro fiber towel, rain boots, light rain coat, small umbrella, electronic adapters

Skype set-up for parents; make sure all is working before you go

Make copies of ALL documents—passport, driver's license, credit/debit card, travel documents, plane tickets, hotels, hostels, AAA card

Travel bag: Sucrets, cough drops, Tylenol, Benadryl, Tums, Bacitracin, Neosporin, Visine, Purell, band-aids, Carmex, Vaseline, Ponds dry skin cream, Dove lotions, soap, shampoo, conditioner, Vick's VapoRub, Q tips, deodorant, perfume, toothpaste/brush

Suitcase: pack one small one with a small amount of clothes that give you many combinations

Pack date

Dates leave and return

Assigned dates when the student will contact you so you can have peace of mind. I recommend once a week on a set day and time at least.

When figuring costs, the items I calculated included: food (daily, weekly, monthly), pubs, tuition, fitness and fencing clubs, travel, lodging, gifts, and spending money.

Planning extensively beforehand makes the trip that much more enjoyable for both the parent and the student, especially if this is the first time your student has been far from home.

Chapter 32
How You Can Make
It Special Week By Week

Below are some of the cards, messages and care packages I sent. Please use what works for you to make it your kids' special memory.

One great resource I found was Napkin Notes. Garth Callaghan was diagnosed with kidney cancer when his daughter Emma was 12. He wanted to make sure she knew she mattered, so he wrote one note for every day to be included in her lunchbox until she graduated. That touched my heart, and I included many of his messages in my cards. His notes can be found at 21daysofthankfulness.com, and they have also been published in *Napkin Notes*.

I also found encouragement in Joel Osteen's book *I Declare*. Check out page 68.

Ideas to send in the once-a-month care package include:

- A card. I try to buy in advance so I have a stack; you just need to make sure you didn't already send the same one.

- A picture of me pointing to my eyes with another picture of me pointing back to her with the caption, "I'm watching you from under your roommates' bunk bed." Okay, I never did it, but what a great idea for freshman year!

- Stickers

- Candyland's big tub of popcorn for her and her five roommates

- Mail order Shari's Berries for her and her five roommates (berries.com)

- O & H Danish out of Racine, Wisconsin. You can find them at ohdanishbakery.com.

- Flowers that smell really good

- Chocolate

- Money

Okay, here are some cards that I sent to our girls during college. Use what you want from them, but at least you have some foundation instead of trying to come up with something all on your own for each and every week like I did. Tip: Once you have the freshman year done, you can copy and paste them in a different order for the next year or as a similar situation comes up. Don't forget to add those little surprises of Napkin Notes, quotes that will resonate with them, and of course CASH inside the card (who doesn't appreciate a little dough-ray-me cold hard coin to go out and do something with?).

Freshman Year

I had two girls in college at the same time and at the same school, so I've commingled cards. I also included $20 cash and postage stamps so they could write me back. Ha! In a Word document, I kept a description of the card I sent each daughter along with a copy of my note. That way I could make sure I didn't send the same daughter the same card twice, and I could use some of my quotes and notes over again in later years.

Week 1

CARD

"You have what it takes; adversity can bring out the best in people, and that's certainly true of you." Inside: "Your courage is an inspiration."

WHAT IT SAID

Well, it's been about one week of you being up there and getting prepared for your first year. WOW, how exciting of a time in your life this is, and boy is time ever going by fast! Hope you and your roommate are all settled and that you have found some new friends up there. If I know you, you'll have about three or four of them within your first day. Ha, ha! Make sure you have your routine in place for studying, dance, fun and of course REST!

Glad you got your package and that you LOVED the pictures. It took me about 20 minutes to decide which, if any, I should get for your walls. Enjoy the rest of it, and I thought it would start out your first year well.

Too bad that you could not keep the room as we had it, but you are so positive with it, that it made me very PROUD of you! Ran across this article and thought it had a lot of good points that both you and your sister could utilize. Be well, stay strong and positive, and remember we LOVE YOU, but don't come home too soon! Dad

Week 2

WHAT IT SAID

Congrats on your very successful move. You are off on another one of life's adventures. Make this year the best one yet. I am so proud of you! You are turning into quite the young adult/woman! You worked hard; that shows me you have drive and want more for your life.

You have picked great friends and that tells me you have good character judgment. Now, remember to set the proper routine for success; study hard, get great grades, really apply yourself so you can get a great and exciting career (not a job that is boring), develop great friendships and life experiences, perform exceptionally at your sport and be the leader you are. You need to keep in mind that I have eyes and ears everywhere, and there

*is very little that I don't know. So, you need to ask yourself this question:
what would my all-knowing, bright, intelligent, extremely protective dad
say? If I would say yes, then you can say yes. Wait. I mean if your normal,
level-headed, in-his-right-mind dad would say yes, then you can say yes. If
it is the other dad, then you had better run for the hills, hide the women
and children and batten down the hatches. Ha, ha! Better yet, you had
better ask your mother!*

*Mom said you needed some things for your walls, and I picked these up.
If you don't like them, no big deal. See if your sister or someone else would
like them. They were only a dollar each. Also, thought you girls would like
some treats while you work out, study and have some down time.*

*Remember to check your mail box often for I just might find the time,
energy and desire to send you things from time to time. I can't say you will
like them if and when I do, but one never knows. Ha, ha! I LOVE YOU. Dad*

Week 3

WHAT IT SAID

*You don't call, write, text, and you did not come down to the State Fair
to visit me in the Education building while I was working at the CSB/SJU
booth. I mean, a lot of your friends did and fellow dance team members. I
was crushed, hurt and beside myself, not knowing where the love went or
why it left. So, I got you your own screen cleaner that I especially saved for
you as they went like wildfire. Ha, ha! I know you are busy having a blast,
and that is what it is all about, especially your first year. Stay COOL, study
hard, play and rest. LOVE you, Dad.*

Week 4

WHAT IT SAID

*It sure was great to see you both and I am glad you both really enjoyed the
Taylor Swift concert. It made for a wonderful weekend. I know Mom really
enjoyed having you there and for breakfast and talk time. Even Sashay
was pleasantly surprised to see you both. Even though she has become
Mom's new sleeping partner/cuddler and my morning companion even*

more so. Ha, ha! Your brother needs some sister beat-up time as well, from what I heard, for he gets enough from me.

I am sending you $20 so you can go out and buy some cards and stamps to write your good old dad a card, note, etc., and not an email. Mail me a note once in awhile, even though I know you'll go out and blow it on something else. I can hope, can't I? LOVE YOU very much. Dad

Week 5

WHAT IT SAID

Keep up the great effort on all fronts, classes-attending, homework-actually doing, studying-applying yourself, dance-giving it your all, friends-one can never have enough or do enough with, and whatever else occupies your time. Ha, ha! Love you and PROUD of you! Dad

Week 6

CARD

Little girl on her bike with a doll house, "Congrats on your move!"

WHAT IT SAID

[I sent her this because she wanted to go back to St. Ben's—her new HOME. Also sent HOME stickers for her to put up.]

Week 7

WHAT IT SAID

It was sure great being with you this past weekend even if it was only for a short time. Yet, the time we spent together over lunch was even better. I LOVE seeing you so happy being up there and being yourself, expanding your wings, flying free to make your own decisions and experiencing LIFE! This can be a life-changing event, and I hope you enjoy it to its fullest and get a lot out of school, sites, experiences, new worldly friendships, etc. Sure do love you and am PROUD of you! Dad

Week 8

WHAT IT SAID

[Sent her $20 plus stamps to write her dad a card and not an email.]

Week 9

WHAT IT SAID

Happy Halloween to you and your fellow mistresses of the night. Sending you a little Halloween décor for your place so you can have a scary atmosphere plus some other fun items. Carpet cleaner so your room smells fresh and sweet. A good reading article as an FYI from a LOVING and CARING DAD. So, please read and ponder. LOVE you tons! DAD

Week 10

WHAT IT SAID

I'll be picking you up tonight, and I cannot wait to hear all about your Madison trip. I am proud of you for finding what is important to you, and please keep up the talks so when you need my input, I can be there for you. You will make the right decisions, and some not so right decisions; it is how you deal with the good times as well as the bad times that makes us who we are. My only hope for you is to be happy and enjoy each stage of your life as best it can be. Sounds like everything is coming together on all fronts.

Keep it up and remember, I am here anytime you need me. Love you.

Week 11

CARD

"Amazing Woman"

WHAT IT SAID

I saw this card and immediately thought of you! You rock girl, you're amazing as it states and I am so PROUD of you! Hope this brightens your day and makes you smile as you read it. LOVE you, Dad

Week 12

CARD

Bicycle on it with flower basket

WHAT IT SAID

Hey honey, saw this card and had to get it for you. Plus a really cool portable calculator for those times you are in need of a small portable calculator. Lest I forget, some nice Halloween socks so you are styling around school, town and, of course, your dorm. Plus a LOT of breakfast bars so you start your days off GREAT! LOVE you, Dad

Week 13

WHAT IT SAID

Thanks for the great card. You have no idea how much I like getting them. You most certainly found one that fits me as well. How did you know? Ha, ha! Glad you're loving the packages and cards that I send your way. Being the envy of others is a good thing as long as you are sharing. Ha, ha! Hope you made those Halloween socks rock! Glad you liked them. Hope you are having a great day and week. Love you, Dad

Week 14–Care Package

CARD

Cat sitting on bed holding books with pillows all around him—Purrfect!

WHAT IT SAID

Wow, it is your first ever Finals Survivor Care Package from your good old father, mother, brother and Sashay. This is meant to help you through all those late night study sessions where you may forget to eat, drink and shower. So, with this package, I am giving you high octane energy stuff, some air freshener to keep you and your roommate in a livable manner, and some great holiday season items.

It's starting to look like Christmas around here; oh wait, with this latest package, now it can start to look like Christmas. Enjoy all of the goodies, study hard, test GREAT, and do your best. That is all we can ask of you. This is a fantastic time of your life. So, now's the time to buckle up and get busy, but also have some fun. So, you keep studying, and I've provided the fun. I am very PROUD of you, my daughter. Hope you have a great week. Love you, Dad

Week 14–Care Package

WHAT IT SAID

You should have received your AWESOME finals/holiday care kit by now, and it should start to look a lot like Christmas around there with the starter kit I sent you. These cards will add to the holiday look 'n feel as well. It was great seeing you this weekend. Very PROUD of you.

You are on the team, keeping a positive attitude, and it will all work out in the end. Just stay positive, keep moving forward, and the doors will open up for you soon. I believe in you. Looking forward to seeing you over the holiday and spending some time with you. So, study hard, get GREAT test scores from your GREAT efforts, and come home to relax and take the much needed break you need and deserve. LOVE you very much, PROUD of you! DAD

Week 15

CARD

Cat in a Japanese-like setting

WHAT IT SAID

[Told her Sashay wanted to send her a card; she got HUGE pay for using her picture—unlimited cat nip. Told her getting a plan makes finals easier. I told her everyone was excited about her coming home for awhile, except Christina, the girl who I said I had rented out her room to. I also said we were prepping the ice rink. If things went well, the rink should be good for skating in one to two weeks.]

Week 16

CARD
My life is richer because you're in it

WHAT IT SAID
[How nice it was to have her home for thanksgiving and her wanting to have her friends over. Great to know that we have made our home a safe place for her and her friends.]

Week 17

CARD
Penguin with fabric

WHAT IT SAID
It was awesome having you home for the holidays, playing games with all, catching up, going to the Vegas movie and hanging out. I am sure PROUD of you, what you are up to and how much you are an adult and making very sound decisions! Can't wait for you to come back for Christmas and hope you enjoy your package, if you did get it. Stay warm, study hard, take needed breaks, remember to eat, shower and finish up this semester strong and well. Love you, Dad. P.S. Isn't this an awesome card?

Week 18

CARD
Christmas tree with gold ornaments

WHAT IT SAID
This card ties in quite nicely with all the others I have been sending during this festive month and package you received. Just think, Christmas is almost here; can't you just wait for the gifts? I know you have some great ideas for me and Mom, but keep in mind I don't want any and save your money for what you need and want to do. Just having you home with us is the BEST GIFT you can give me. LOVE YOU, DAD

Week 19

WHAT IT SAID

You are 1/8 the way done with college. How does it feel? What did you learn already? A routine is best to keep things on track and also to have fun.

Week 20

WHAT IT SAID

Congrats on your first semester behind you. Well done, way to go! Take what you learned from the first and apply it to the second. Improve on what worked and change what did not. Now jump in with both feet, your whole body, and shine. I am so proud of you! LOVE, Dad

Week 21

CARD

Red Christmas card with poinsettia look

WHAT IT SAID

Thanks for the BEST Christmas yet, with many more to come. Your gift of dinner being made, movie with treats, and cleaning the house was PERFECT! Especially with all of you joining us at dinner. I really enjoy all of us being together and admire the young adults each of you have become and will continue to be.

It was great being with you, and I am so excited for you with regard to your next life path you are about to partake on and watch what unfolds for you. Truly, it is the best ever with each path getting better than the previous one. Enjoy life and all it has to offer you. Be kind to others, help those in need. Be happy with who you are and what you have. Laugh often, even at yourself. Let no one or no thing take away your happiness. Only you can allow that and nothing should be able to do that. Remember, I LOVE you and am very PROUD of you and BELIEVE in you! You are a wonderful, talented and beautiful woman.

Plus I sent you some goodies to start this semester off right along with some for your roommate and even some ornaments to keep the festivities alive for a bit longer, and you can add to your collection for next year. Love you, Dad

Week 22

CARD
A London-looking girl with hand bag

WHAT IT SAID
Soon you will leave for Florida for another LIFE experience. Traveling with a team is an awesome time and I hope you enjoy it as much as I did. Keep up the great effort and all of your hard work will pay off. Be patient, stay positive and it will all work out. I am so PROUD of you and what you are accomplishing! You should have had some letters and care packages already there for your return from the holidays, and I hope you enjoy them. This card really made me think of you, and I hope you like it. LOVE you, Dad

Week 23

WHAT IT SAID
How you doing? Whatcha doing? Catching up on life with you. Here is a little something to brighten your day or have a coffee, scone or something. $20 bill. Soon you'll be leaving for Florida, and I can't wait to hear how it goes for you. Wishing you all the best and very PROUD of you honey. Dad

Week 24

WHAT IT SAID
Live in the sunshine—congrats on sixth place in Florida's dance competition—how great is that, the best the team has done! Just think of what you will accomplish in the years to come with your experience, input and talent. I am so proud of you.

Week 25

CARD
Way to go!

WHAT IT SAID
Celebrate Good Times! CONGRATS 1st place National Champs! Congrats to you and your team! WOW, how amazing and what an accomplishment to you all. You are now one of the elite to hold this title and honor. I am so PROUD of you and can't imagine how you feel for you have accomplished something I have not. PROUD of you for all your hard work, effort and positive attitude. Can't wait to see you and give you a congrats hug! Until then, here is a little something for you to go out and celebrate! LOVE, DAD

Week 26

CARD
Little girl on a dock looking over the edge with her inner tube, snorkel, mask, and flippers

WHAT IT SAID
"You can do it"—It's another semester and you already have one under your arms. Now jump in with both feet, your whole body, and shine.

Week 27

CARD
Pink card with a yellow phone on it

WHAT IT SAID
Wow, how's this card for timing, and how sparkly is it? It hits the mark on so many levels. Ha, ha! I really enjoyed your card that you sent me. It truly means a lot how much you appreciate all we have and are doing! Both your mom and I are so PROUD of you and the young woman you have become. I cannot wait to hear about what you experience next and what

it means to you. The tradition of the cards and care packages also is a bit more fun for me since I truly feel it makes your day, week or even month. Who knows what the next one will include or when it will arrive. Continue on with your adventures and keep me posted. Love you, Dad

Week 28

CARD
A Valentine's card with package

WHAT IT SAID
You must be special for I wanted to make sure you had this holiday covered as well as the others. Inside you'll find some other necessities that you may like to have and cannot get there or are too expensive. Enjoy and keep in mind, "Personality is everything in art and poetry." How appropriate with where you are being all about art and poetry. Love you and have a great day. Dad

Week 29

WHAT IT SAID
Great talking with you the other day and hearing about what you are up to. Make sure you order your National Championship ring. I am so PROUD of you, Tori! Congrats on your job at school and summer one. Should be a good money making summer for you. Remember, "You're Awesome! True Story!" Love you, Dad. P.S. What did you think of your latest package?

Week 30

CARD
Chinese hand fan on it

WHAT IT SAID
It was awesome spending time with you this past weekend, enjoying some sushi and fried rice. I also enjoyed hearing about your life, dorm, friends,

work and your new boyfriend. Keep doing what you are doing and finding your particular path in life. Don't let anyone, including Mom and I, dictate what you do for yourself. We are only there to give you our insights from past experiences, looking from the outside in, as your friends probably do and you do for them. Ultimately, it is your choice to pursue what makes you happy as long as it is what YOU want, wish, desire, need, crave, etc.

I am PROUD of you and LOVE you very much, my young lady. Keep doing what you are doing and every semester will get better and easier as well as the friendships you have and will continue to make. Remember—"It's what's inside that counts," Dad

Week 31

WHAT IT SAID

Hope you are doing well and things are moving along nicely for your semester. Your Florida vacation is almost here, and I bet you are very excited. Also, Mom let me know about you and [ex-boyfriend], and I hope you are doing okay with it. Remember relationships and friendships will come and go. True love will find you; use all these experiences as learning and self-discovery lessons.

Things work out for the best, and I am very proud of you for standing strong on your decision of being at the college you chose and that you feel it was a great choice. Plus you're developing the great friendships that come with being around campus and materializing these special lifetime friendships. If it is meant to be, it will work out in the end. If not, then you will experience a whole new thing.

Keep in mind that one takes these times as ways to realize what is important to them with regard of how one wants to be treated, talked to and respected/loved and how one will reciprocate those same emotions and feelings. Remember, I am here for you anytime you need someone to talk to either just to listen or offer my advice. I can do either or both and will never fault you for your decisions. Thought this little cuddly thing would help you when in need. Love you, Dad. You're awesome!

Week 32

CARD

A square card with a peacock with a purse

WHAT IT SAID

What a great card for a great daughter. It's unique, just like you. Hope you had a great break and enjoy your classes this semester. Keep up the great work, effort and things will continue to fill your purse. Love, Dad [I put $20 into card/purse. Ha, ha!] You know all those things you wanted to do? You should go do them! What's stopping you?

Week 33

CARD

A big GREAT Dane with a little girl holding the leash

WHAT IT SAID

Okay, since I can't be over there helicopter hovering protecting you, I am sending over my friend BRUNO! He's a no-nonsense kind of guy. Yet, he does have a weakness that I know you'll exploit. Yes, he likes bacon just like me and all kinds of other treats. Once you give him those things, he'll be putty in your hands. Ha, ha!

Hope you are having an AWESOME semester with school, friends and life! Love you, Dad. "Well done is better than well said." ~Benjamin Franklin

Week 34

CARD

A gold dragonfly

WHAT IT SAID

Something pretty and special like you are! Great having you home for the holidays even though I give you a hard time about being home and when are you going back. It just wouldn't be me if I didn't.

I am so very proud of you and LOVE you very much. Dad
Most of us are just about as happy as we make up our minds to be.

Week 35–Care Package

WHAT IT SAID

This care package is meant to be filled with: lots of Easter treats, a
fun night light for you might need it—who knows when, some shower
pampering items to use, in case you need them, toys for you and your
friends to have fun with, and something to help you with your last minute
projects, studying and corrections. Do you think it is big enough for all
those times you might need to use it? Ha, ha! Love you and enjoy.

If you're the smartest person in the room, you're in the wrong room.

Week 36

WHAT IT SAID

Rumor has it that you and your friends are finding your wilder side. Just
remember that Dad knows and is watching with his many eyes. Hope you
are having fun as you get close to the end of your first year in college.
WOW, how fast did that go?

Week 37

CARD

Black cat on bed with books on both sides of its arm and a small book in
its paws

WHAT IT SAID

As it comes down to the wire, the finals preparation begins. Good habits
start with the proper set up, and you could learn from your little friend
here.

First, get all reading materials required and set up so you have limited
movement to go get them (for you may not, in the end, have the energy
to later). Second, prop them up so you expend the least amount of effort

to pick them up. Third, tackle the smallest ones first so you get a sense of accomplishment. Fourth, have back-up relaxation pillows so if you happen to doze off while in the middle, you have a safety catch in place. Five, have plenty of liquids available so you don't get dehydrated and pass out. Finally, a COLD shower always helps when in need. Ha, ha!

Love you and keep up the GREAT work. I'm proud of you.

"Inspiration exists, but it has to find you working." ~Pablo Picasso

Week 38

CARD

Dog hanging onto a hose that read "Hang in there"

WHAT IT SAID

Year starting to wind down and finals soon... Well, it's getting close, your first year is almost done. WOW, how quick was that? Now's the time to buckle up and get busy but also have some fun. So, you keep studying, and I'll provide some fun. Remember, all of us love you and are proud of you! Hang in there. The person who is renting out your room, since I need the discretionary income, will be moving out for the summer and asks if she can leave some of her clothes for next year. Dad

Week 39

CARD

Sent her a congrats card to our home address

WHAT IT SAID

CONGRATS on your first year in college. WELL done, honey! I/we are so PROUD of you! Now, it is time to have some summer fun and make some money for next year. Keep one-quarter for fun spending money, one-quarter for next year's college needs, one-quarter for savings, and one-quarter for college loans this year. Remember, it is meant to be an awesome life experience, and it will be over before you know it.

LOVE you, DAD

Sophomore, Junior, and Senior Years

For my daughters' second, third and fourth years, I sometimes copied and pasted quotes and comments from prior years, so there aren't as many in this section. But I did still send each of them one card a week!

Week 2

WHAT IT SAID

Congrats on your very successful move. You are off on another one of life's adventures, and make this year the best one yet. It's your second year already. My, how fast time is going by! Love your new digs as well. It should be a BLAST! I am so proud of you! You are quite the young lady! You worked hard this summer. That shows me you have drive and want more for your life. Enjoy your friends and gather up even more this year. Experience the community at night and on weekends like never before to make this year even more memorable.

Now, remember the proper routine for success you established these past years: study hard, get great grades, really apply yourself so you can get a great and exciting career (not a job that is boring), develop great friendships and life experiences, perform exceptionally at your sport and be the leader you are. This year especially only concentrate and focus on what is current and the future will fall into place. Also, make sure you sign up for those liberal arts classes: painting, pottery, photography, etc. With how AWESOME you are at these things, it will be a great way for you to enjoy some classes and excel. What a great way to recharge your batteries and forget about the other classes. I LOVE YOU. Dad

Week 2

WHAT IT SAID

It's been about two weeks of you being up there and getting prepared for your fourth year. WOW, is time ever going by fast. Soon you'll be back home living here till we are old and gray. Ha, ha!

Hope you and your roommates are all settled, you have your routine in

*place for studying, fun and of course REST! I am glad to hear that you did
get your package and that it hit the mark for you. Some fun stuff to leave
messages for the guys next door, on the walkway, or just passersby. Who
knows what you will come up with? Be well, stay strong and positive and
remember we LOVE YOU, but don't come home too soon! Ha, ha! Dad*

Week 3

CARD

Oriental symbol with a fish. "May the beauty of your day bring
happiness and simple pleasures."

WHAT IT SAID

*It's been about two weeks of you being up there and getting prepared for
your second year.*

*So happy for you and your new job at the COFFEE shop. I knew you'd
love it, and I can't imagine all the people you'll meet doing it as well. Be
well, stay strong and positive, and remember we LOVE YOU, but don't
come home too soon! PROUD of you. Ha, ha! Dad*

Week 4

WHAT IT SAID

*It was sure great being with you this past weekend and learning about
the exciting once-in-a-lifetime trip to London you'll be participating in. I
can't wait to see and hear all about it while you are there and when you
get back. This can be a life-changing event, and I hope you enjoy it to
its fullest and get a lot out of school, internship, sites, experiences, new
worldly friendships, etc. Sure do love you and am PROUD of you! Dad*

Week 5

CARD

Says "Thinking of you"

WHAT IT SAID

Pretty much says it all, doesn't it? Oops, it doesn't say "I Love YOU,"
though. Heard you had some good appointments for job hunting. Keep it
up and relax; it will all come into place as it needs to and when it is time.
Enjoy your last year and all your lifelong friends. Until I see you then,
LOVE, Dad
P.S. Now you have to admit this is an awesome card and envelope, too.

Week 6

CARD
An Italian cafe

WHAT IT SAID

Doesn't the picture make you want to go out to a dinner? Found all kinds
of fun stuff for you and your roommates to have fun with. You don't need
to ask them to scratch your back anymore though; I gave you something.
Ha, ha! The pandas made me laugh and thought they would you too.
*   Flash drives to save all that important stuff you are working on. Love*
you, Dad

Week 6

WHAT IT SAID

It was great going to a movie with you last night. I really enjoy hearing
about what you are up to and what's going on with your life. Sounds like
everything is coming together on all fronts. Keep it up, and remember, I
am here anytime you need me. Love you.

Week 6

WHAT IT SAID

Loved your Halloween pictures of you as dolls! Well done! Hope you are
having a great day and week. Here's some dough-ray-me for you to have a
cup of java or ? Guess you will be coming home soon, but I guess I can deal
with it. Love you, Dad

Week 7–Care Package

CARD
Halloween mask card

WHAT IT SAID
It's time for a PACKAGE, yes, PACKAGE time for you. Halloween is an awesome package time, and you'll find some nice little fun things and treats for you. Plus some fun knick knacks as well. Enjoy this holiday, be safe and be smart. You know I'd not be your dad if I did not say that. LOVE you and PROUD of you honey.

Week 8

WHAT IT SAID
I am very PROUD of you, and it was amazing seeing you and the event, and I had no idea what it was all about. So glad I went to experience it and see how much you blossom during it. What you have accomplished during your dance career is more than many, and only a few have been so rewarded as you have! Yet, this life path has come to an end to allow for another life path to open up and prosper by you and your efforts. Now, have fun and really enjoy this last semester of your college career. Love you, Dad

Week 9

CARD
Girl in pink with a crown on her head. Inside reads, "You are an amazing, inspiring, beautiful warrior princess; stay strong and carry on!"

WHAT IT SAID
I am PROUD of you! I LOVE you! You are AMAZING! You are TALENTED! You are BEAUTIFUL! You will do GREAT things in life!

Week 9

WHAT IT SAID

*Great having lunch, coffee and chatting with you the other day.
I am so PROUD of you, and just remember to focus on what is truly
important at each moment in time and let other things go versus trying
to take on so much by yourself and feeling overwhelmed. If it is meant to
be, it will be. If not, it is for the better. As my friends tell me, remember to
BREATHE. Have a great day and enjoy your gifts and the FREE coffee that
awaits you. Love, Dad*

Week 9

CARD
Valentine's card

WHAT IT SAID

Wishing you a very special day. I love you! Dad

Week 10

CARD
Boy with Mohawk wearing a swimsuit on the beach with the caption
"How you doing?"

WHAT IT SAID

*Hey you, yeah, I'm talking to you! How you doing? Just chilling out,
catching some rays, reading (okay pretend-reading a good book), and
checking things out. So, How R U doing?*

*I love this card! It's so me! Just had to send it. Got your card and I
loved it, meant a lot to me thanks, and I'd like very much to come up and
spend time with you. Will try to set up as things settle down with all life's
craziness. Yet, GOD only gives us what we can handle. Guess I can handle
a lot. Yes, I am so PROUD of you! It's great to see you so happy! Knowing
you made a wise decision and life's going well. Have a great day and
CHILL! Love you, DAD*

Week 10

WHAT IT SAID

*Loved your Halloween pictures of you as Katy Perry and your better half
as a Kitty. Not sure why he was the kitty, but he pulled it off. Ha, ha! Never
did get the pictures of you both being insurance agents though and was
looking forward to seeing those. Send them my way. You made those
Halloween socks rock. Glad you liked them.*

   Hope you are having a great day and week. Love you, Dad

Week 10–Care Package

WHAT IT SAID

*Wow, time is winding down quickly and this is getting near to being the
last CARE package I am sending to you. Thought you and your mates
would love to have some goodies, treats, snacks, food like items. The Easter
Bunny dropped some things off for me to give to you. I tried to keep some,
but he/she—NO one knows, wouldn't let me. Oh yeah, some fun things as
well. You know how AWESOME bunny ears are. If you don't, well, you soon
will. LOL, LOVE you TONS. Dad*

Week 11

CARD
"A Special Hello"

WHAT IT SAID

*It was GREAT seeing you this weekend, and I LOVED your dances! I think
you and your team will do well this year. Also, Mom and I were very happy
to see how happy you are being there! It is a wonderful thing to see that
you are enjoying it as much as we did.*

   *Maybe more...but not too much. Ha, ha! Wanted to send you a bunch of
stuff. Enjoy! Love you, Dad*

Week 11

CARD
Pop-out globe with flowers on it

WHAT IT SAID
Thought you'd LOVE this card for it truly is different and UNIQUE as you are! I am so PROUD of you and how you are handling all that occurred during these tough times! The way you are able to separate things into what is right versus wrong also is impressive. How you stand up for those who cannot or those who need your help against the wrong/bad/evil is why we are all here. I know it is tough, but it is making you stronger and into the remarkable women that you are! Stay positive and all will keep moving forward. Love you, Dad

Week 12

WHAT IT SAID
It was great seeing you this weekend, and I am so PROUD of what you are doing with your Prep School dance team! The song was PERFECT along with the costumes and the dance; well, what can I say about that that has not already been said! Looking forward to seeing you over the holiday and spending some time with you. So, study hard, get GREAT test scores from your GREAT efforts and come home to relax and take the much needed break you need and deserve. LOVE you very much. PROUD of you, DAD

Week 12–Care Package

CARD
In pink glitter: "You are AMAZING"

WHAT IT SAID
WOW, your senior year is almost over! How exciting for you! I know it is a bitter sweet thing, happy/sad, awesome and scary all in one. I am so PROUD of you, and this will be an incredible year of life experiences being

made. Your future is about to materialize and unfold in front of your very own eyes. All you can do is your very best at each moment in time, hold onto the memories, and capture the feelings as they occur. Press on positively and don't hold your breath, for you may miss something truly incredible. This will be your last COLLEGE care package from me, but hey, save all those for when you do (if you do and your mom lets you) move out. LOL. Now off to the races so to speak, my eldest daughter! Love you tons! Dad

Week 13

CARD
Says "Marvelous, Fabulous, Wondrous/It's all about us."

WHAT IT SAID
[Sent her a sticker that says "Good Times" and a loofah.] I thought you needed something to help keep you clean; good times in the shower. Ha, ha! Enjoy and have a great day. Love you, Dad

Week 15

CARD
Bear saying "Sending you a little hug"

WHAT IT SAID
Just thought you could use a nice bear hug from your good old dad today. Hope all goes well for you this week. Love you lots. Dad

Week 15

CARD
Christmas card with snow flakes

WHAT IT SAID
Well, your first London card and maybe many more to come? It depends

on how much you need them, want them, appreciate them or how often you FaceTime me on my cell phone. Ha, ha! I know this is an exciting time for you and hope it is everything you hope it to be. It is truly a life experience that not many get to experience and all of us will be living vicariously through you.

Take lots of pictures; send us lots of emails on what you are doing so we can feel a part of it. Study hard, do well in school first and foremost for that is why you are there. Know this, I am very PROUD of you, BELIEVE in you, LOVE you and wish you all the best. I have heard that it is expensive there, so I hope this $20 allows you to have some extra food for the week, day—okay, meal. Ha, ha! Dad

Week 16

CARD
Die-cut flower pick with yellow inside

WHAT IT SAID
Enjoy your hodge podge of gifts this week. I heard that you needed a fan, and I did buy this before we brought you the real one, but this one plugs into your computer so you can have it at your desk. Pretty darn cool if you ask me. Also, I found some knick knacks that I thought you'd enjoy. Have a great week and I guess we'll see you soon again for you just keeping coming back. Why? Ha, ha! I love you!

Week 17

WHAT IT SAID
It sure was great to FaceTime with you last week, see you and hear your voice. Not to mention seeing your flat. Wow, is this an exceptional opportunity for you and I am so happy for you. To see you so happy makes me smile. Keep in mind that while you are over there, don't not do something just to save pennies in the scheme of life. Mom told me about a trip that was only a couple hundred dollars and that's okay to do once in awhile, especially when all are going. We don't want you to be too smart

and penny conscious; but also don't be too willing to do everything as well. Trust your smarts and do what you feel is right. When in doubt, by all means call us to discuss, and we'll help you as much as we can.

Mom and Grandma are super excited about coming to see you and I am excited for all three of you. It will be a great time I think, and I can't wait to see and hear all about it as well.

Did you get your package I sent? Not sure how that goes versus a letter, but it is a lot of work to send. Hope you like what I included in it. Love you so very much and make sure you study hard, get good grades first and foremost. The fun and good times will be there as well. Take in the sites and keep that BLOG up to speed so I know what you are doing, where you've been and can see the sites for myself. Love you, Dad

Week 18

CARD
Pink card with yellow phone

WHAT IT SAID
Wow, how's this card for timing? I really enjoyed our FaceTime call this Sunday at 6 a.m. my time and noon your time. Yet, I was tired for good reason and did not sleep until noon. Ha, ha! I am so glad you are so happy with this life experience you are in right now. It truly is a gift to be able to do this and what memories you are creating not only for yourself but your mother and I as well.

I so look forward to reading your updates on your BLOG, but the FaceTime is truly a blessing to be able to capture your feelings live! Just think how difficult it was for those in the past when this technology was not available and the parents would have to wait for a letter so long in between or a very expensive phone call.

The tradition of the cards and care packages also is a bit more fun for me since I truly feel it makes your day, week or even month. Since things are so expensive over there or not available. Who knows what the next one will include or arrive?

Continue on with your adventures and keep me posted. Also, I sent you two quick, easy, cheap and feeds-a-lot recipes (Chicken a la King and Beef Stroganoff) on your phone. Did you get them, did you make them, and what did your flatmates think? Love you, Dad

Week 19–Care Package

CARD
Kitty hanging by claws on rope

WHAT IT SAID
First, we all want to say how PROUD we are of you! All of us are and even the cat, for she posed for this great card for you. We know firsthand how demanding finals can be on your time, mind and energy level. Hang in there, you CAN do it! We all also thought that you'd ENJOY this GREAT CARE package filled with all kinds of goodies and fun things to CHEER you up, brighten your day and think of us. ENJOY them a little bit each day as you need them and know that we are rooting for you! Go! Love you, from your good old dad! But don't let anyone know that I am. Ha, ha!

Week 19

CARD
Valentine's Day package and separate card

WHAT IT SAID
Wow, two packages relatively close together. You must be special. I wanted to make sure you had the holidays covered while away since all of your cartons for holiday decorations are back here. Not to mention some other necessities that you may like to have and cannot get there or are too expensive. Enjoy and keep in mind, "Personality is everything in art and poetry." How appropriate since where you are is all about art and poetry. Love you, and have a great day. Dad

Week 20

CARD

Waterfall with "I know you're dealing with a lot right now, and I just want you to know that it's going to work out" on the front. Inside: " I believe in you."

WHAT IT SAID

[Sent three holiday stampers and three paper stickers.] As finals get closer along with all of your other activities of dance, coaching, etc., I know things can seem to be a bit much. Just know that you'll do GREAT with all of them, and I believe in you very much. Thought these FUN things would add to your care package we sent. Enjoy them. LOVE, Dad

Week 20

CARD

Papyrus card with hummingbird in foil

WHAT IT SAID

Great FaceTiming with you the other day and hearing all about your continued adventure. Sounds like you have a good game plan, and it's not surprising that changes are occurring for that is what travel is all about. New ideas and things to consider. I know you can't wait to really get out and experience the sites, but it will be well worth the wait to have most of it occur at the end versus a little bit here and there. You'll remember all the last parts more for they'll be fresh in your mind.

It sounds like you'll not only experience overseas travel, but some sites within the good ole U.S.A. as well as see your significant other who, I know, will love the surprise. Keep up your positive attitude, have fun with your internship and don't forget to send me some shopping links of stuff to buy for you-oops, I mean your mom that she'll never wear—Ha, ha! Love you, Dad

Week 21

WHAT IT SAID

My oldest, here are some more items for the 12 days of Christmas that I thought you'd enjoy for this holiday season. Have fun and do well on your finals. We'll see you home soon, and I am looking forward to our night out together on Wednesday. Love you, Dad

Week 21

WHAT IT SAID

It was awesome reading your latest BLOG! WOW, how the time is flying by for us, can't imagine how it is for you. Love the updates, pictures and how you write/capture the mood, setting, experience. It's as if I am there with you. You are very talented that way. Can't wait to hear about your internship and your travels when they start. Envious of all the fish 'n chips you are experiencing! I would love to have some from there. Can only imagine how most excellent it is!

Also, glad you are enjoying your letters and packages. Yet, sharing is something you need to work on from what I read. Yeah, right. Ha, ha! I am PROUD of you and LOVE you very much, my young lady. Keep doing what you are doing and every semester will get better and easier as well as the friendships you have and will continue to make. Dad. Remember—It's what's inside that counts.

Week 22

CARD

Outside: "Hello" Inside: "How's one of my favorite people doing today?"

WHAT IT SAID

It seems like yesterday that you were back home. Wait a minute, it was just yesterday. Ha, ha! So, how is one of my favorite people doing today? It's a new semester, and I hope it is a GREAT one for you. I sure am proud of you and really have enjoyed watching you become the young lady you are and all the GREAT decisions you are making. Oh yeah, [boyfriend] is a good decision as well. Yet, I still need to have my talk with him. Yet, the talk just might not be as necessary as it once was for obvious reasons. I guess my plan has worked all these previous years. See all the bad dates and guys I saved you from! I love you, Dad

Week 23

CARD

Four girls in gowns on cover with words "Stylish, Sophisticated, Intelligent, Fabulous"

WHAT IT SAID

I saw this card and can't believe that they described me so well on the cover with the words "Stylish, Sophisticated, Intelligent, Fabulous." Yet, they had a picture of four women on it? Ha, ha! Wanted to say it was great having you home over the holidays, meeting [boyfriend] and seeing you so happy. Wishing you a GREAT new semester of learning, doing well in dance, experiencing life and having fun. LOVE you, Dad

Week 23

WHAT IT SAID

The AWESOME life experiences continue on with your latest stop to Paris. Wow, how great was that? Can't wait to read and hear all about it, and see pictures of Ireland. It is a place I've always wanted to go to, to stay in an old time castle, walk the wide open plush green land, experience the pubs, etc. So, your BLOG will be allowing me to have some of that experience. I am so happy for you, my young beautiful lady/daughter, and am so excited for you. With that being said, thought you and your flatmates would enjoy some popcorn for movie night(s), animal crackers for you. Did I send enough this time? Ha, ha! Love you.

Week 24

CARD
Italian cafe table with umbrella. Outside: "Thinking about you and how much I enjoy our lighthearted little chats." Inside: "Let's get together soon."

WHAT IT SAID
As the card does say on the outside, I do very much enjoy our lighthearted chats! That goes without saying and is profound. However, on the inside is where I am having difficulty. "So let's get together soon"? That pretty much has me on the fence, on the ropes or simply saying, not sure how to respond. Though I do enjoy your company, I also enjoy you being away. Ha, ha! I know you know that I do miss you, and this is just our little banter going back 'n forth. With all of that being said, hope your new semester is going well, and I am sending you a little fun item to light your way in the dark. Enjoy and I LOVE you.

Week 25

CARD
Puppy with a heart collar [really, it's a Valentine's day card]. Inside: "There's nobody sweeter than you! Wishing you lots of love."

WHAT IT SAID
What a cute and cuddly card for my very sweet daughter. Wishing you a great day, honey! Love you, Dad

Week 25

WHAT IT SAID
This might be your last care package to London I send so you and your flatmates had better enjoy it. I have included lots of Easter treats. Love you and enjoy.

Week 26

CARD

Outside: "Happiness is not a state to arrive at, but a manner of traveling."

WHAT IT SAID

When I saw this card, I just had to get it and send it to you along with all of those things that can bring one to the happiness state by traveling with fun! So, enjoy your bingo game with your friends, don't forget to share with them the ring pops and when you are in need of some fairy dust, just put together your puzzle. Ha, ha! Love you tons, Dad

Week 26

CARD

Congrats card

WHAT IT SAID

WOW, both of you on the same team at the same time. How exciting this year will be, and we can't wait to watch you both together. It will be a great year and one to remember filled with many awesome memories for you both! LOVE and PROUD of you both.

Also LOVED my birthday card; it is awesome! Finish up your semester strong and then off to your post travels where you'll gain some incredible life experiences and memories as well as finishing it up with a life time trip to visit and surprise [boyfriend]. So PROUD of you and am here anytime you need me.

Most of us are just about as happy as we make up our minds to be.

Week 27

CARD

Hippie era amoebas

WHAT IT SAID

[Sent chocolates and Blow Pops] Thought you and your roomies might enjoy some candy to start your day. The card is pretty neat as well. Should be a very nice addition to your collection. Hope you are having a great day and week. Guess we'll be seeing you later on this week for you are coming home yet again. Ha, ha! See you soon and LOVE you tons. Dad

Week 27

WHAT IT SAID
Welcome home, and it is good to have you back safe and sound. Can't wait to hear all about your adventures and see all the amazing pictures. Here are some left over global postage stamps that I thought you might want to use for sending letters to your significant other. One per envelope. Love you honey! Dad

Week 28

CARD
A picture of famous "people who probably didn't think of you today."

WHAT IT SAID
[Sent Play-doh] I saw this card as I was thinking of you and just had to buy it and send it to you to let you know who was not thinking of you today. Ha, ha! Plus, I then saw this fun dough for you and your roomies to play with. So, have fun and know that I am thinking of you today. Love, Dad

Week 29–Care Package

WHAT IT SAID
Wow! I am super excited to see your finished art work soon and hope you have one set aside for me to enjoy at office or at home! You are really shining in your creative element, and I am so happy for you for finding an area that you are truly talented in and seems to come naturally for you. Thought you and your friends would love to have some goodies, treats, snacks, food like items in this CARE package. LOVE you TONS. Dad

Week 30

CARD

A pop-out globe with flowers on it

WHAT IT SAID

Thought you'd LOVE this card for it truly is different and UNIQUE as you are! I am so PROUD of you and how you are handling all of life's trials and tribulations that are coming your way. It is making you stronger with each one and, I know it is hard to believe, it will get much better soon. Remember, when one door closes, another opens. This too shall pass. What was meant for my harm only makes me stronger. Stay positive and all will keep moving forward. All of us are 100 percent behind you, and we will do what we can to right the wrongs.

With regard to your pottery, I had better get one for my office, and I do like the far end one on right. Just saying. LOL! Love you, Dad

Week 31–Care Package

WHAT IT SAID

Hi, my wonderful daughter who sent me the most FANTASTIC birthday care package ever! WOW, how did you learn and know how to send such a wonderful thing? Ha, ha! Back atcha; I am sending you some fun things to brighten your day: Girl Scout cookies (your faves), water balloons so you can have fun tossing them at your friends, bubbles—just because they are bubbles, and, of course, your dad's personalized pen. The sound quit though, but you can just imagine what it does. LOVE you TONS. Dad

Week 32–Care Package

CARD

Boy by the ocean with his hands in the air. Caption: "Yes, you can do it!"

WHAT IT SAID

[Sent $20 and postage stamps so she can write me and others back. Ha,

ha!] As it comes down to the wire, the finals preparation begins. I thought you'd enjoy one of my Finals Care Packages sent a bit early.

So, now's the time to buckle up and get busy, but also have some fun. So, you keep studying, and I've provided the fun. Finally, a chocolate-covered rose to tell you how much I love you and how proud I am of you. Plus you can eat it; it's chocolate, for Pete's sake. Wait. Who's Pete?

I/we are so PROUD of you! Keep it going and have fun. It will be over before you know it. LOVE you

Week 33

WHAT IT SAID

WOW, it is the end of your second year of college. My, how fast indeed it is going and has it been eventful for you! Yet, you have met each challenge as a CHAMPION has and does, which only tells me how STRONG you truly are! Keep it up and things will definitely go your way.

This will be your last package for this year, and I hope I got some things that will make your studying for finals go easier. I will leave you with these words of wisdom; I am PROUD of YOU! I LOVE you! You are AMAZING! You are TALENTED! You are BEAUTIFUL! You will ACCOMPLISH GREAT things in LIFE! Keep doing what you are doing. Stay POSITIVE. Now off to your next adventure in your life. I'll see you soon and bring you home for the summer. Do the best you can, and that's all we can ask of you. LOVE you TONS! DAD

Appendix

A—Cruise Tips

My wife and I have been on three cruises: two by ourselves and one with our whole family. Over the course of these cruises, I have found the following things to be very helpful in ensuring we get the full experience.

What to Bring (outside of the usual):

- Walkie talkies with about 40 channels and extra batteries. Bring one for each person traveling with you. It's a great way to find out where everyone is and what they are doing versus trying to find them on the ship. Plus, when some people go offshore to different events, you can touch base as well. Cell phones don't typically work on ships especially while out at sea.

- Cash is king for tipping; there are about five different roles that receive tips, and they typically give you envelopes to do so. This is really the only substantial money that the help get and they depend on it. Also, positive comments go a long way. We always tried to meet and talk to some of the help. We found them to be a great resource of what to do and what not to do on each excursion.

- Cameras. An underwater cover is a great idea along with video cameras, cell phones, computers and chargers, if you plan on bringing them.

- Binoculars

- Backpack for off-ship excursions

- Ziplock bags for keeping wet things separate and protecting items from water or sand

- Minimal baggage. Generally just bringing one small bag per person is best because the cabins are small.

- Incidentals: a small umbrella, insect repellant, motion sickness meds, small flashlight

- SCUBA gear

- Bottled water. If you buy before boarding, you can save money. (Same thing with liquor.)

- Gift list of those for whom you want to shop

- For safety's sake, you might want to also bring a door lock bar and a salt water converter. And when we travel, we put only my work address on our bags, not our home address.

A few tips for an even better cruise:

- Find the maître d and try to arrange for dinner at the captain's table. These book up early and we've heard they are awesome, but we've never had the chance to do one.

- The purser desk can arrange tours of the kitchen, galley, bridge, and food demos, etc.

- The concierge can plan all items in advance for you: massages, hair appointments, excursions, shows, dinner seating times—a later time allows for more time on shore excursions, and a $20 tip goes a long way—and special events like renewing wedding vows with the captain (we did this and it was AWESOME), a tour of the bridge and galley, or having strawberries, flowers and champagne delivered to your room as a surprise.

- When off ship, bargaining with street vendors is what it is all about. They feel the first sale of the day sets the pace and will bargain much more then. So, get to them early and have fun.

- Get a ship credit card.

- Plan for early check-out midway through the cruise so you don't have to spend an extended period of time waiting in line. Just pack up and leave.

- You can wash some clothing in the cabin sink using hot water/soap and laundry detergent, and then hang the items up to dry in the shower.

- Pay with a credit card so you can dispute the charges in case something happens.

- Call credit card companies ahead of time to let them know where you will be traveling.

B—Camping 101

Listed below are things that I found helpful to plan, pack and have with when going camping. This list is very similar to what I would bring to hockey camp and tournaments, too, sans the hockey gear.

Clothes

Swimsuits	Tee shirts	Sandals
Goggles	Sweat pants	Rain gear
Towels	Shirts	Umbrella
Shorts	Socks	
Jeans	Tennis shoes	

Food

Food (duh!)	Napkins, towels	Gas grill and extra gas
Cooler and ice	Pots, pans, utensils	Cooking stove, gas
Beverages	Bowls, mixing	Condiments
Butter tub and sticks	Tupperware	Garbage bags
Plastic silverware	Ziplock bags	
Heavy duty plates	Tinfoil	

Tent

Tent, tool set, spikes	Pillows	Sound machine
Ropes	Blow up mattresses	Clip-on lights
Sleeping bags	Extension cords	
Blankets (a lot of them)	Fan, heater	

Leisure Activities

Game Boy, games	Books	Baseball glove, ball, bases
Batteries	Magazines	
Board games	Sun, reading glasses	Baseball bat, tee ball stand
Cards	Suntan lotion	Kick ball
Bocce ball	Bikes, scooters, and helmets	Golf clubs, shoes
Croquet		

Miscellaneous Items

Shaving kit	Portable radio	Dishwashing soap
Cell phones	Lanterns	Lighter
Chargers	Hats	S'more sticks
Cameras, photo,video	Laundry basket	Fold out chairs
Bug spray	Plastic bins	3 gel ice packs
Flashlights	Wood, paper, lighter	
Walkie talkies	Bowl, clean dishes	

Menu

Menu plan before you go. Here are some easy items to make while camping.

Eggs	Meat on the grill	Popcorn, butter, salt
Salads	Deli meat	Pancakes with syrup
Baked potatoes	S'mores	
Peanut butter and jelly	Fruit	

C—Graduation Party Tips

After having gone through this a few times, I consider myself an expert at planning graduation parties. According to Ginger Venable, who wrote *Graduation Parties: Everything You Need to Know from Start to Finish*, the average cost of an open house is $1,200. So you definitely want to make it memorable and perhaps less expensive than average.

For a unique graduation open house, think about starting with a theme that goes beyond the school and its colors. Pool party? Dunk tank? Have a food truck on site like a taco, French fry, or ice cream truck? Maybe you choose a different location such as a picnic pavilion in the park.

Make the food interactive so it helps people mingle. Fajitas, tacos or pizzas (with pre-made crusts) are great ideas.

Here are my cost saving tips:

- If you want to avoid doing a full meal, choose a late morning or mid-afternoon start time for your party.

- Ask relatives and friends to help by bringing a tray of bars or a bag of chips. Return the favor when it's their turn to host an open house.

- Choose one unique aspect to your party (photo booth, game, food truck, etc.) instead of three or more.

- Have a group party instead of a party for one individual. If you do this, decide how many people each person gets to invite.

- You can buy a case of 240 cookies for between $30–$43 at Best Maid Cookie Outlet.

- Helium-filled balloons can be ordered from Party City for between 89 cents and three dollars each. They often sell out. Dollar stores also often carry them for, you guessed it, one dollar.

- Price check at the warehouse clubs like Sam's Club and Costco. They may have the best deals on items like flowers, food, paper products, deli trays, cakes, cookies and bars, and these can be bought in bulk.

- Graduationparty.com has more information, too. Great resource!

- Instead of a disc jockey, consider hiring a school friend who has a band.

To organize this, I created an excel spreadsheet to track what needed to get done, when it got done, and the cost of various items. For example, I listed out how many tents I thought we would need and what we wanted to hang in them for ambiance like lights. I also included how many tables and chairs, along with stand-up cocktail tables, we would want.

D—The Annual Hockey Party Potluck

So, what does one do when one has a portable hockey rink in their back yard? Well, they have parties; a lot of them!

This section shows you how to invite, what to plan for and what to do.

My first rule, because I don't want to worry about the boys taking each other out with hard hits, is everyone will bring all gear and wear it. So now you and I don't need to worry.

The actual invitation is listed below. I emailed it to every participant and made it potluck so it shared the burden. Katie didn't have to stress out because she didn't have to do anything. Doesn't get any easier than that now does it?

The invite was emailed so all attendees could simply "reply all" so nobody doubled up on items, and you will end up with something that will shoot and score with each kid and you won't have to shop for, cook or clean up every dish. And use paper products for easy clean-up.

Keep track of who you invited, their email addresses, who can make it, and what food is being brought.

Done deal! You're all set, and you can now sit back by the fire pit with drink in hand and enjoy watching them play while enjoying good conversation and making new memories!

You're Invited to The Annual Kubinski Backyard Hockey Party

Date: Phone:

Time: 1pm till 6pm   RSVP:

Place: Kubinski's home

What to do:

- Hockey game in all your gear

- Boot hockey

- Snow ball fights

- Sit by the fire

- S'more fire fun

- Kick back, relax and look at some really cool Christmas lights. I did it myself, Griswold-like.

- Good conversation

- Indoors: basketball game, video games, dance contest, etc.

What to bring:

- Skates and your kids' full hockey gear

- Warm clothes for s'more and fire fun

- One item for potluck

Potluck Choices

Please pick one and let us know (we can let you know if it's been chosen already):

We're planning on about 16+ adults and 20+ kids

Pop	Beer	Appetizer
Juice boxes	Wine	Second appetizer
Chips and dessert	Main dish	Plates, cups
Second dessert	Second main dish	Silverware, napkins
S'more goodies	Third main dish	

Notes

Notes

Notes

_____

_____

_____

_____

_____

_____

_____

_____

_____

_____

_____

_____

_____

_____

_____

_____

_____

_____

_____

_____

Epilogue

Our families, kids and significant others are truly blessings from God, so cherish them, love them and have FUN with them more often than not. It will be these things they remember and talk about with their friends and later their own families.

As I have told my kids, it's the great circle of life. (Yes, I stole this from *The Lion King*.) Each of them will hold in their hearts things that their mother and I have done. They will bring these things to their families. No one is perfect or does everything they way they would have wished. We all have said, "When I get older, get married, have kids, etc, I am never doing...."

From one parent to another, let me reaffirm what I consider some key tenets of parenthood:

It is my God-given right, duty and privilege to put the FEAR of God into each and every man who wishes to date my daughters. Don't ever take that away.

It's my duty to embarrass my children as much as I can; it's my way of showing them just how much I love them.

Protect them when you need to!
Fight the battles you need to fight on their behalf.
Let them fight the ones that they need to.
Let them grow and blossom.
Don't be a helicopter parent!
Signed, Papa Kubs (Speedo) AKA Tom Kubinski